The Online Money Maker: A Comprehensive Guide to Making Money Online

Residual streams of income can help you expand your earning potential and reach financial independence goals more quickly

Wesley H. Adams

Table Of Contents

01

Chapter 1: Introduction to Making Money Online

Understanding the Potential of Making Money Online

In today's digital age, the internet has revolutionized the way we live our lives. From communication and entertainment to shopping and business, the online world has become an integral part of our daily routine. But did you know that it also holds immense potential for making money? This subchapter will delve into the endless opportunities available to you in the online realm and guide you on your journey to becoming an online money maker.

One of the most popular ways to make money online is through affiliate marketing. This entails promoting products or services on your website or social media platforms and earning a commission for every sale made through your unique affiliate link. With the right strategies and marketing techniques, you can generate a significant passive income stream.

Another lucrative avenue is freelancing. If you possess a specific skill set, such as graphic design, writing, or programming, you can offer your services to clients worldwide. Freelancing allows you to work on your own terms and monetize your expertise while enjoying the freedom of working remotely.

Dropshipping is yet another exciting opportunity to explore. By partnering with suppliers, you can set up an online store and sell products without having to worry about inventory or shipping. This business model offers flexibility and scalability, enabling you to expand your product range and reach a global customer base.

Online tutoring is gaining popularity as more students seek personalized learning experiences. If you have expertise in a particular subject, you can provide virtual tutoring sessions and help students achieve their academic goals. This rewarding endeavor not only allows you to make money but also contributes to the personal development of others.

Social media management has become a vital aspect of businesses' marketing strategies. If you have a knack for creating engaging content and building online communities, offering social media management services can be a lucrative venture. You'll help businesses enhance their online presence, increase brand awareness, and ultimately drive sales.

Blogging and content creation are excellent options for those passionate about writing and sharing knowledge. By creating valuable content and attracting an audience, you can monetize your blog through advertising, sponsored posts, or even selling digital products or courses.

Online surveys and market research provide an opportunity to make money by providing valuable insights to companies. By participating in surveys or testing products, you can earn rewards or cash and contribute to the development of new products and services.

Virtual assistant services are in high demand, as many entrepreneurs and busy professionals require support with administrative tasks. By offering efficient and reliable virtual assistance, you can build a thriving online business. Lastly, e-commerce and online store management have become more accessible than ever. With platforms like Shopify, you can set up your own online store and sell physical or digital products, allowing you to tap into a global market.

In conclusion, the potential of making money online is limitless. Whether you choose affiliate marketing, freelancing, dropshipping, online tutoring, social media management, blogging, online surveys, virtual assistant services, or e-commerce, there are abundant opportunities waiting for you. This subchapter has only scratched the surface of what is possible, but armed with the right knowledge and determination, you can embark on a rewarding journey to becoming an online money maker.

In today's digital age, making money online has become increasingly popular and accessible. The internet offers countless opportunities for individuals to earn a substantial income from the comfort of their own homes. However, like any venture, there are both benefits and challenges associated with making money online. In this subchapter, we will explore these aspects and provide insights for those interested in pursuing online income streams.

Benefits and Challenges of Making Money Online

One of the most enticing benefits of making money online is the flexibility it offers. Unlike traditional 9-to-5 jobs, online money-making allows individuals to set their own schedules and work at their own pace. This flexibility is especially appealing to those seeking a better work-life balance or individuals with other commitments. Whether you are a stay-at-home parent, a student, or someone looking to escape the corporate world, making money online provides the freedom to work on your own terms.

Another significant advantage is the ability to reach a global audience. Unlike brick-and-mortar businesses, online ventures are not limited by geographical boundaries. This opens up a vast market of potential customers, giving you the opportunity to expand your reach and increase your earning potential. Whether you are involved in affiliate marketing, dropshipping, or selling digital products, the internet allows you to tap into a worldwide customer base.

However, it is important to note that making money online also comes with its fair share of challenges. One of the main obstacles is the ever-changing nature of the internet. Staying up to date with the latest trends and algorithms is crucial for success. Online platforms and algorithms are constantly evolving, making it essential to adapt your strategies accordingly. This requires continuous learning and staying ahead of the curve, which can be a challenge for some.

Another challenge is the potential for scams and fraudulent activities. With the rise of online money-making opportunities, there has also been an increase in scams and schemes. It is crucial to exercise caution and thoroughly research any opportunity before investing time or money. Being aware of red flags and utilizing trusted platforms can help mitigate these risks.

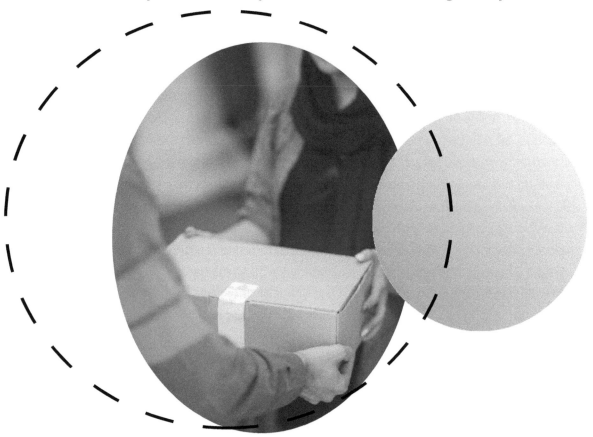

In conclusion, making money online offers numerous benefits, including flexibility and a global reach. However, it is important to be aware of the challenges that come with it, such as staying updated with industry changes and avoiding scams. By understanding and overcoming these challenges, individuals can unlock the vast potential of online income streams in various niches such as affiliate marketing, freelancing, dropshipping, and many more.

Setting Realistic Expectations and Goals

In today's fast-paced digital world, more and more people are turning to the internet to make money. Whether you're looking to supplement your income or create a full-time online business, setting realistic expectations and goals is crucial for your success. In this subchapter, we will explore the importance of setting achievable targets and how it can drive your online money-making journey forward.

When it comes to making money online, it's easy to get caught up in the hype and promises of overnight success. However, it's essential to approach this endeavor with a realistic mindset. Understand that building a sustainable online income takes time, effort, and dedication. By setting realistic expectations, you can avoid disappointment and stay motivated throughout your journey.

One of the first steps in setting realistic expectations is to assess your skills, interests, and resources. Identify your strengths and weaknesses and find online money-making opportunities that align with your abilities. Whether it's affiliate marketing, freelancing, or dropshipping, choose a niche that you are passionate about and have the necessary skills to excel in.

Next, set specific and measurable goals. Instead of aiming to "make a lot of money," break it down into smaller, achievable targets. For example, if you're starting a blog, set a goal to publish two high-quality blog posts per week and increase your website traffic by a certain percentage each month. These actionable goals will help you stay focused and track your progress effectively.

It's also crucial to be aware of the time and effort required to achieve your goals. Making money online is not a get-rich-quick scheme. It takes consistent effort, continuous learning, and adapting to the ever-changing digital landscape. Be prepared to invest time in acquiring new skills, building your online presence, and nurturing your audience or customer base.

Additionally, don't forget to celebrate your milestones along the way. Recognize and reward yourself for achieving smaller goals, as this will boost your motivation and help you stay on track.

In conclusion, setting realistic expectations and goals is vital for anyone looking to make money online. By understanding your skills, setting measurable targets, and acknowledging the effort required, you can navigate the online money-making journey with confidence and determination. Remember, success is not guaranteed overnight, but with dedication and perseverance, you can create a sustainable and rewarding online income in the long run.

02

Chapter 2: Getting Started with Affiliate Marketing

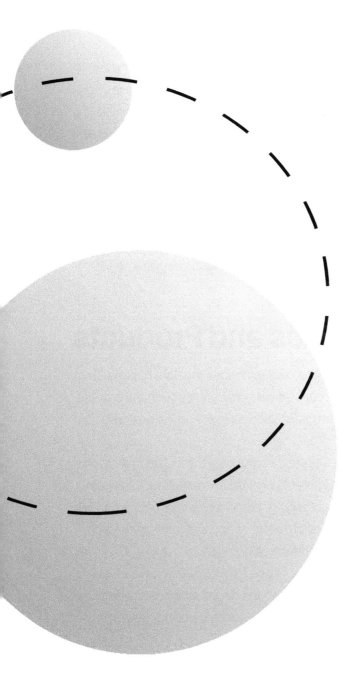

Introduction to Affiliate Marketing

Affiliate marketing is a powerful and lucrative method of making money online. It has become increasingly popular among individuals seeking to generate passive income or even start their own online businesses. In this subchapter, we will introduce you to the fundamentals of affiliate marketing and how you can leverage its potential to create a successful online venture. Affiliate marketing is essentially a partnership between a merchant and an affiliate, where the affiliate promotes the merchant's products or services and receives a commission for every sale or lead generated through their efforts. It is a win-win situation for both parties involved. The merchant gains exposure and increased sales, while the affiliate earns money without having to create their own products or deal with customer service.

One of the key advantages of affiliate marketing is its flexibility. As an affiliate marketer, you have the freedom to choose which products or services to promote. This allows you to align your efforts with your interests and expertise, making the process more enjoyable and effective. You can select from a wide range of niches, such as fashion, health and wellness, technology, or even digital products like e-books or online courses.

To become a successful affiliate marketer, it is crucial to build a strong online presence and establish trust with your audience. This involves creating valuable content that educates and engages your target market. You can leverage various online platforms, such as websites, blogs, social media, or email marketing, to promote the merchant's offerings and drive traffic to their website.

Furthermore, understanding the importance of effective marketing strategies is essential. This includes search engine optimization (SEO), paid advertising, email marketing campaigns, or even influencer collaborations. By continuously optimizing your marketing efforts, you can increase your chances of generating higher conversions and earning substantial commissions.

In this subchapter, we will dive deeper into the intricacies of affiliate marketing, exploring topics such as choosing the right affiliate programs, creating engaging content, driving targeted traffic to your offers, and maximizing your earnings. Whether you are a beginner looking to dip your toes into the world of affiliate marketing or an experienced marketer seeking to enhance your skills, this subchapter will provide you with valuable insights and practical tips to excel in this dynamic industry.

By harnessing the potential of affiliate marketing, you can unlock a world of opportunities to monetize your online presence and achieve your financial goals. So, let's embark on this exciting journey together and discover the limitless possibilities of affiliate marketing.

Choosing Profitable Niches and Products

In the vast world of online money-making opportunities, it is crucial to choose the right niche and product that aligns with your interests and goals. This subchapter will guide you through the process of selecting profitable niches and products that will set you up for success in the online business arena.

Making money online offers a plethora of options, and it's essential to identify the niches that resonate with your skills, passions, and expertise. Whether you're interested in affiliate marketing, freelancing, dropshipping, online tutoring, social media management, blogging, content creation, online surveys and market research, virtual assistant services, selling digital products or courses, or e-commerce and online store management, this guide will help you make informed decisions.

To begin, it's vital to research and analyze each niche thoroughly. Look for niches that have a high demand but low competition. Consider the profitability potential and the target audience's willingness to spend money in that specific niche. Utilize keyword research tools to identify popular search queries and gauge the level of interest within a particular niche.

Once you have identified a niche or multiple niches that have potential, it's time to delve into product selection. Research and identify products that are in-demand and align with your chosen niche. Look for products that offer a unique selling proposition and differentiate themselves from competitors. Consider the quality, price, and potential profit margins of the products you're considering.

Furthermore, it's crucial to assess the competition within your chosen niche. Analyze your competitors' strategies, pricing, marketing tactics, and customer reviews. Identify gaps in the market and opportunities to offer something different or better. This will help you position yourself effectively and stand out from the crowd. Additionally, consider the scalability of your chosen niche and product. Will it allow you to expand and diversify your business in the future? Can you leverage your skills and expertise to create additional income streams within the same niche?

Lastly, don't forget to consider your own skills, interests, and passions when selecting a niche and product. Passion and enthusiasm for your chosen niche will fuel your motivation and dedication to succeed.

By carefully choosing profitable niches and products, you are setting yourself up for success in the online money-making world. This subchapter has provided you with the necessary tools and insights to make informed decisions and embark on a profitable online business journey. Remember, thorough research and analysis, coupled with your own passions and expertise, will pave the way to a thriving online venture.

Building a Website or Blog for Affiliate Marketing

In the digital age, one of the most profitable ways to make money online is through affiliate marketing. This subchapter will guide you through the process of building a website or blog specifically for affiliate marketing, enabling you to maximize your earnings and establish a successful online business. Firstly, it is crucial to choose the right niche for your website or blog. Consider your target audience and their interests. You want to select a niche that aligns with your expertise and passion, as this will make it easier to create high-quality content that engages your readers.

Once you have identified your niche, it's time to create your website or blog. Start by choosing a reliable hosting provider and registering a domain name that reflects your chosen niche. Next, select a user-friendly content management system (CMS) such as WordPress, which offers a wide range of customizable themes and plugins to enhance your website's functionality. When designing your website or blog, prioritize simplicity and user-friendliness. Opt for a clean and professional layout that is easy to navigate. Ensure that your website is responsive and mobile-friendly, as an increasing number of people access the internet through their smartphones.

Content is king in the world of affiliate marketing, so focus on creating high-quality, informative, and engaging content for your audience. Regularly publish well-researched articles, product reviews, and how-to guides that provide value to your readers. Incorporate relevant keywords to enhance search engine optimization (SEO) and attract organic traffic to your website.

To increase your chances of success, it's essential to build a loyal and engaged audience. Interact with your readers by responding to comments and questions promptly. Consider incorporating social media integration to encourage sharing and engagement on platforms such as Facebook, Twitter, and Instagram.

Finally, monetize your website or blog by strategically placing affiliate links within your content. Ensure that these links are relevant and add value to your readers' experience. Be transparent about your affiliate partnerships to maintain trust with your audience.

By following these steps, you can build a website or blog that is optimized for affiliate marketing. With dedication, consistency, and a focus on delivering value to your audience, you can create a profitable online business in the exciting world of affiliate marketing.

Creating High-Converting Affiliate Marketing Strategies

Affiliate marketing has emerged as one of the most popular ways to make money online. With its low start-up costs and potential for high returns, it has attracted individuals from various niches, including making money online, freelancing, dropshipping, online tutoring, social media management, blogging and content creation, online surveys and market research, virtual assistant services, selling digital products or courses, and e-commerce and online store management. If you are looking to maximize your affiliate marketing efforts and generate high conversions, this subchapter provides valuable insights and strategies.

Firstly, understanding your audience is crucial. Research and identify your target market's pain points, needs, and desires. By aligning your affiliate products or services with their requirements, you increase the likelihood of conversions. Utilize surveys, social media analytics, and online forums to gather data and create buyer personas that represent your ideal customers.

Secondly, building trust and credibility are paramount in affiliate marketing. Engage with your audience through blog posts, social media, and email marketing. Share valuable content, offer expert advice, and demonstrate your expertise in the niche. By establishing yourself as a reliable source of information, your audience will trust your recommendations and be more inclined to purchase through your affiliate links.

Next, consider diversifying your affiliate marketing strategies. While promoting products or services through blog posts and social media is effective, exploring additional avenues can yield better results. Experiment with email marketing campaigns, webinars, podcasts, or even creating your own digital products to supplement your affiliate income.

Furthermore, mastering SEO techniques is essential for driving organic traffic to your affiliate links. Optimize your website or blog with relevant keywords, create compelling meta descriptions, and ensure your content is user-friendly and shareable. By ranking higher in search engine results, you increase your chances of attracting potential customers and boosting conversions.

Lastly, continuously track and analyze your affiliate marketing efforts. Monitor click-through rates, conversion rates, and revenue generated from each affiliate campaign. Identify the strategies that yield the best results and optimize accordingly. Additionally, stay updated with industry trends and adapt your strategies accordingly to stay ahead of the competition.

In conclusion, creating high-converting affiliate marketing strategies requires a deep understanding of your target audience, building trust and credibility, diversifying your approach, mastering SEO techniques, and constantly analyzing and optimizing your efforts. By implementing these strategies, you can maximize your affiliate marketing potential and generate substantial income in your chosen niche.

03

Chapter 3: Freelancing: Building a Sustainable Online Career

Introduction to Freelancing

Freelancing has become a popular and viable option for individuals seeking financial independence, flexible work hours, and the ability to work from anywhere in the world. In this subchapter, we will delve into the world of freelancing and explore how it can become a lucrative venture for those interested in making money online.

Freelancing refers to the practice of offering services or skills on a project basis to various clients or companies. It allows individuals to work independently without being tied down to a traditional 9 to 5 job. The freelance market is vast and diverse, offering opportunities in a wide range of niches such as writing, graphic design, programming, social media management, virtual assistant services, and more.

One of the key advantages of freelancing is the ability to choose the type of work you want to do. Whether you possess expertise in a particular field or have a passion for a specific niche, freelancing allows you to leverage your skills and interests to find clients who are willing to pay for your services.

Another appealing aspect of freelancing is the flexibility it offers. As a freelancer, you have the freedom to set your own work hours, decide how much work you want to take on, and even choose your clients. This level of autonomy allows you to create a work-life balance that suits your needs and preferences.

Furthermore, freelancing provides an excellent opportunity to earn a substantial income. With the increasing demand for online services, businesses and individuals are constantly seeking talented freelancers to meet their needs. By marketing yourself effectively and delivering high-quality work, you can attract clients and steadily increase your earnings.

In this subchapter, we will guide you through the essential steps to get started in the freelancing world. We will explore how to identify your skills and niche, build a strong online presence, create an attractive portfolio, and effectively market yourself to potential clients. We will also discuss the importance of networking, managing client relationships, and establishing a solid reputation as a freelancer.

Whether you are looking to make freelancing your full-time career or simply want to earn some extra income on the side, this subchapter will equip you with the necessary knowledge and tools to succeed in the freelancing world. So, let's explore the exciting world of freelancing and discover how it can be your gateway to financial freedom and professional fulfillment.

Identifying Marketable Skills and Services

In today's digital age, the opportunities for making money online are endless. Whether you're looking to supplement your income or start a full-fledged online business, it's crucial to identify the marketable skills and services that can help you achieve your financial goals. This subchapter will guide you through the process of discovering and capitalizing on your unique talents in the online world.

One of the most popular ways to make money online is through affiliate marketing. By promoting other people's products and earning a commission on each sale, you can leverage your existing online presence or start a new niche-focused website. Identifying your areas of interest and expertise will allow you to select the right products to promote and attract the right audience.

Freelancing is another viable option for generating income online. Whether you possess graphic design, writing, programming, or marketing skills, there's a high demand for freelancers in various industries. Identifying your niche and honing your skills will help you stand out in a competitive market, allowing you to charge higher rates and secure consistent work.

Dropshipping is an increasingly popular e-commerce model that requires minimal upfront investment. By partnering with suppliers, you can create an online store and sell their products without ever handling inventory. Identifying trending products and mastering marketing techniques will be crucial to your success in this field.

Online tutoring has gained significant traction in recent years, especially with the rise of remote learning. If you have expertise in a particular subject, you can offer your services as an online tutor. Identifying the subjects you excel in and targeting specific student demographics will help you build a reputable tutoring business.

Social media management is a highly sought-after skill in the digital marketing realm. Companies are willing to pay top dollar for individuals who can effectively manage their social media presence and engage with their target audience. Identifying your strengths in social media platforms and staying up-to-date with the latest trends are essential for success in this niche.

Blogging and content creation offer a multitude of opportunities to monetize your skills and knowledge. By identifying your passions and areas of expertise, you can establish yourself as an authority in your chosen niche. From sponsored posts to affiliate marketing, there are various ways to monetize your blog and content.

Online surveys and market research offer a simple way to make money online. By sharing your opinions and participating in market research studies, you can earn cash or rewards. Identifying legitimate survey websites and dedicating time to complete surveys regularly can provide a steady source of income.

Virtual assistant services are in high demand as more businesses are transitioning to remote work. By identifying your organizational and administrative skills, you can offer your services remotely to businesses or entrepreneurs. From managing emails to scheduling appointments, your assistance can be invaluable to busy professionals.

Selling digital products or courses is an excellent way to leverage your expertise and knowledge. Whether it's an e-book, online course, or digital artwork, identifying your area of expertise and creating high-quality digital products can generate passive income.

E-commerce and online store management is a lucrative field for those with an entrepreneurial spirit. By identifying profitable niches and sourcing in-demand products, you can create a successful online store. Mastering inventory management, customer service, and marketing strategies will be essential to your long-term success.

Identifying your marketable skills and services is the first step towards making money online. By understanding your strengths, passions, and areas of expertise, you can carve out a profitable niche in the digital world. Whether it's through affiliate marketing, freelancing, or e-commerce, the opportunities are endless – it's up to you to seize them.

Creating a Freelance Portfolio and Personal Brand

In the highly competitive online marketplace, building a freelance portfolio and establishing a personal brand are essential steps towards success. Whether you are a freelancer, an affiliate marketer, a dropshipper, or any other online entrepreneur, your portfolio and personal brand will serve as your identity and differentiate you from the rest. This subchapter will guide you through the process of creating a powerful portfolio and cultivating a unique personal brand that will attract clients and customers from your target audience.

First and foremost, your freelance portfolio should showcase your skills, expertise, and accomplishments. It should highlight your best work, whether it is related to content creation, social media management, online tutoring, or any other niche you specialize in. Include samples of your work, testimonials from satisfied clients, and any certifications or awards you have received. The portfolio should be visually appealing and easy to navigate, allowing potential clients to quickly assess your capabilities.

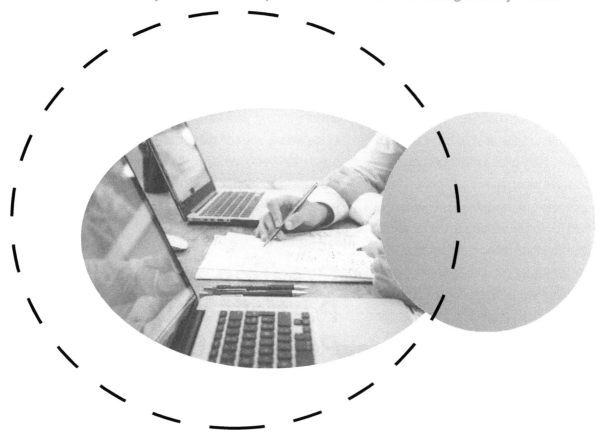

While your portfolio showcases your work, your personal brand represents who you are as a professional and what you stand for. Define your unique selling proposition (USP) and identify your target audience. What sets you apart from others in your niche? What value can you provide to your clients or customers? Develop a compelling brand story that resonates with your audience and communicates your expertise and passion. Consistency is key when it comes to personal branding, so ensure that your brand elements, such as logo, color scheme, and tone of voice, are consistent across all your online platforms.

To establish your personal brand, leverage social media platforms and professional networking sites. Engage with your target audience by sharing valuable content, participating in relevant discussions, and showcasing your expertise. Position yourself as an authority in your niche by creating informative blog posts, hosting webinars, or offering free resources. By consistently delivering value, you build trust with your audience and increase your chances of attracting clients and customers.

Lastly, continuously update and refine your portfolio and personal brand. As you gain more experience and expertise, add new projects and achievements to your portfolio. Stay updated with industry trends and incorporate them into your personal brand. Seek feedback from clients and customers to ensure that your portfolio and brand are effectively meeting their needs.

By investing time and effort into creating a compelling freelance portfolio and personal brand, you will establish yourself as a professional in your niche and attract clients and customers who value your expertise. Remember, your portfolio and personal brand are your key assets in the online marketplace, so make them stand out from the crowd.

Finding and Winning Freelance Jobs

In today's digital age, more and more individuals are seeking ways to make money online. One of the most popular and flexible options is freelancing. Whether you have a specific skill set or simply enjoy working on various projects, freelancing can provide you with the freedom and financial stability you desire. However, finding and winning freelance jobs can be a daunting task if you don't know where to start. This subchapter aims to guide you through the process, ensuring you have the necessary knowledge and tools to succeed in the online freelancing world.

Firstly, it is essential to identify your niche. With numerous opportunities available online, narrowing down your focus will help you stand out from the competition. Whether it's writing, graphic design, coding, or social media management, understanding your strengths and passions will enable you to target the right clients and projects. Additionally, investing time in building a strong portfolio or website showcasing your work will increase your credibility and attract potential clients.

Next, it's crucial to explore various freelancing platforms and job boards. Platforms like Upwork, Freelancer, and Fiverr offer a wide range of freelance jobs across different industries. By creating a compelling profile and effectively showcasing your skills and experience, you can increase your chances of being hired. Additionally, networking on social media platforms such as LinkedIn and joining relevant freelance communities can expose you to hidden job opportunities and potential clients.

To win freelance jobs, you must master the art of crafting persuasive proposals. Tailoring your pitch to each client's needs, demonstrating your understanding of their project, and highlighting your unique selling points will significantly increase your chances of getting hired. Moreover, maintaining clear and professional communication throughout the hiring process is vital in building trust and strong client relationships.

Lastly, it is essential to continuously learn and adapt to market trends. The online freelancing landscape is ever-evolving, and staying up-to-date with the latest industry practices and tools is crucial for long-term success. Additionally, seeking feedback from clients and constantly improving your skills will help you stay ahead of the competition and attract higher-paying freelance jobs.

In conclusion, finding and winning freelance jobs requires a strategic approach. By identifying your niche, building a strong portfolio, exploring various freelancing platforms, crafting persuasive proposals, and continuously learning and adapting, you can position yourself as a valuable asset in the online freelancing world. Remember, freelancing offers immense opportunities for personal and financial growth, so embrace the challenge and embark on your journey to becoming a successful online money maker.

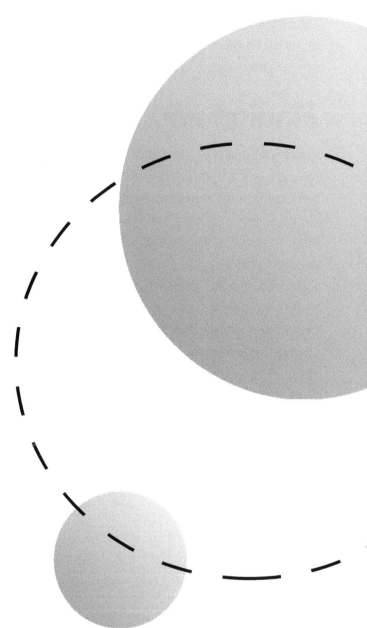

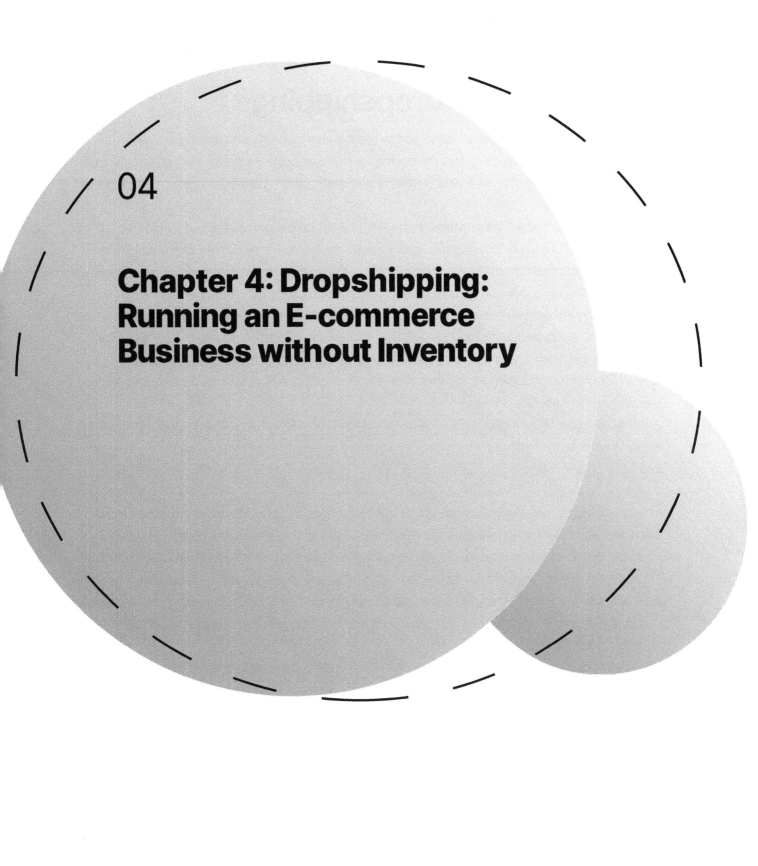

04

Chapter 4: Dropshipping: Running an E-commerce Business without Inventory

Introduction to Dropshipping

In today's fast-paced digital world, the opportunities to make money online are endless. One such lucrative avenue is dropshipping. If you're looking for a flexible business model that requires minimal upfront investment and offers a high potential for profitability, then dropshipping might be the perfect fit for you.

Dropshipping is a retail fulfillment method where online entrepreneurs can sell products to their customers without actually stocking the items themselves. Instead, they partner with a supplier or wholesaler who takes care of inventory management, packaging, and shipping. As a dropshipper, your primary role is to focus on marketing and customer service.

One of the key advantages of dropshipping is its low barrier to entry. Unlike traditional retail businesses that require significant capital to purchase inventory, a dropshipping business can be started with just a laptop and an internet connection. This makes it an ideal option for aspiring entrepreneurs who are looking to dip their toes into the world of e-commerce without taking on substantial financial risks.

Another benefit of dropshipping is the freedom and flexibility it offers. As a dropshipper, you have the ability to work from anywhere in the world, as long as you have an internet connection. This means you can run your business from the comfort of your own home, from a coffee shop, or even while traveling.

In this subchapter, we will delve deeper into the world of dropshipping. We will explore the various steps involved in setting up a dropshipping business, from finding the right niche and selecting reliable suppliers to building a user-friendly website and implementing effective marketing strategies. Throughout this subchapter, we will provide practical tips, proven strategies, and real-life examples to help you navigate the dropshipping landscape successfully. Whether you're a seasoned entrepreneur or a beginner, this subchapter will equip you with the knowledge and tools needed to start and grow your own profitable dropshipping business.

So, if you're ready to embark on an exciting online venture that has the potential to generate a steady stream of income, join us as we dive into the world of dropshipping and discover the endless possibilities it offers for making money online.

Finding Profitable Products and Suppliers

In the fast-paced world of online money making, one of the key factors that determines your success is finding profitable products and reliable suppliers. Whether you are delving into the realms of affiliate marketing, dropshipping, or selling your own digital products, the right products and suppliers can make all the difference in your journey towards financial freedom.

When it comes to finding profitable products, thorough market research is crucial. Understanding the demand and trends in your niche is the first step towards identifying products that have the potential to generate substantial profits. Look for products that are in high demand but have low competition, as this will give you a greater chance of success.

Affiliate marketing is a popular method of making money online, and finding profitable products to promote as an affiliate is paramount. Look for products with high commission rates and a proven track record of conversions. Additionally, choose products that align with your target audience's needs and interests to increase the likelihood of making sales.

For those venturing into the world of dropshipping, sourcing reliable suppliers is crucial. Look for suppliers with a strong reputation and positive customer feedback. It's important to establish a good relationship with your suppliers to ensure smooth operations and timely deliveries. Thoroughly vet any potential suppliers and request samples to assess the quality of their products before committing to a partnership.

If you are considering selling your own digital products or courses, it's essential to produce high-quality content that provides value to your customers. Conduct market research to identify the needs and pain points of your target audience, and create products that address these issues. Additionally, consider leveraging platforms like Udemy or Teachable to reach a wider audience and boost your sales.

Regardless of the online money-making niche you choose, social media can be a powerful tool for finding profitable products and suppliers. Join relevant groups and communities, engage with industry influencers, and stay updated on the latest trends. Additionally, consider utilizing online surveys and market research tools to gather valuable insights about your target audience's preferences and needs.

In conclusion, finding profitable products and suppliers is a crucial aspect of making money online. Thorough market research, building relationships with reliable suppliers, and staying updated on industry trends are all key components of success. By investing time and effort into finding the right products and suppliers, you can greatly increase your chances of achieving financial success in the online world.

Setting Up an Online Store for Dropshipping

If you are interested in making money online and want to explore the world of e-commerce, dropshipping can be a lucrative option for you. This subchapter will guide you through the process of setting up an online store for dropshipping, enabling you to start your own successful venture in the e-commerce industry.

One of the first steps in setting up an online store for dropshipping is to choose a niche. Look for a product category that aligns with your interests and has a high demand in the market. Conduct thorough research to identify potential competitors and ensure that there is enough room for you to establish yourself.

Once you have chosen a niche, it's time to select a platform for your online store. Consider popular e-commerce platforms such as Shopify, WooCommerce, or BigCommerce, as they offer user-friendly interfaces and a wide range of features to help you manage your online store effectively. Next, you need to find reliable suppliers for your dropshipping business. Look for suppliers that offer competitive prices, high-quality products, and efficient shipping services. Websites like AliExpress, Oberlo, and SaleHoo can help you connect with trustworthy suppliers.

After finalizing your suppliers, it's time to customize your online store. Choose an appealing theme that represents your brand and product niche. Ensure that your store's design is user-friendly, mobile responsive, and optimized for search engines. Add product descriptions, images, and pricing details to make your store visually appealing and informative. Marketing your online store is crucial for success. Utilize various digital marketing strategies such as social media marketing, search engine optimization, content marketing, and influencer collaborations to drive traffic and increase sales. Utilize social media platforms like Facebook, Instagram, and Pinterest to showcase your products and engage with potential customers.

To ensure smooth operations, consider integrating automation tools and plugins to manage inventory, process payments, and handle customer inquiries efficiently. Offer excellent customer service to build trust and gain repeat customers. Continuously analyze sales data, customer feedback, and market trends to optimize your product offerings and marketing strategies.

In conclusion, setting up an online store for dropshipping requires careful planning, research, and execution. By selecting a profitable niche, choosing a suitable platform, finding reliable suppliers, customizing your store, and implementing effective marketing strategies, you can create a successful online store and generate a steady income from dropshipping. Remember to stay up-to-date with industry trends and continuously adapt your strategies to stay ahead in the competitive e-commerce landscape.

Managing Orders, Shipping, and Customer Service

In today's fast-paced world, where online businesses are booming, it is essential to have a solid understanding of managing orders, shipping, and customer service. These three aspects play a crucial role in the success of any online venture. Whether you are involved in affiliate marketing, dropshipping, or e-commerce, mastering these skills is vital to ensure customer satisfaction and repeat business.

When it comes to managing orders, organization is key. Implementing an efficient order management system will help you keep track of incoming orders, process them promptly, and provide timely updates to your customers. This system should allow you to easily access customer information, track inventory levels, and generate invoices. By streamlining this process, you can avoid delays, minimize errors, and ultimately improve customer experience.

Shipping is another critical component of running an online business. Choosing reliable shipping partners and negotiating favorable rates can significantly impact your bottom line. It is essential to carefully package and label your products to prevent damage during transit. Additionally, offering multiple shipping options and providing tracking information to customers will create a sense of transparency and trust.

Customer service is the backbone of any successful business. Promptly addressing customer inquiries, concerns, and complaints is essential to building a loyal customer base. Active communication channels, such as email, chatbots, or phone support, should be readily available to cater to customer needs. Training your customer service team to be empathetic, responsive, and knowledgeable will go a long way in resolving issues and creating a positive brand image.

Furthermore, leveraging customer feedback is crucial for continuous improvement. Encourage customers to leave reviews and ratings, and be open to constructive criticism. By actively listening to your customers, you can identify areas for improvement, refine your processes, and stay ahead of the competition.

In conclusion, managing orders, shipping, and customer service are integral aspects of running a successful online business. By mastering these skills, you can ensure smooth operations, enhance customer satisfaction, and drive growth. Whether you are engaged in affiliate marketing, dropshipping, or running an e-commerce store, investing time and effort into these areas will pay dividends in the long run. Remember, happy customers are the key to making money online.

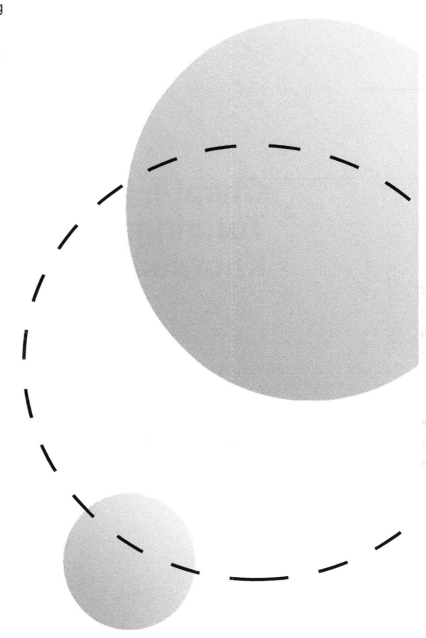

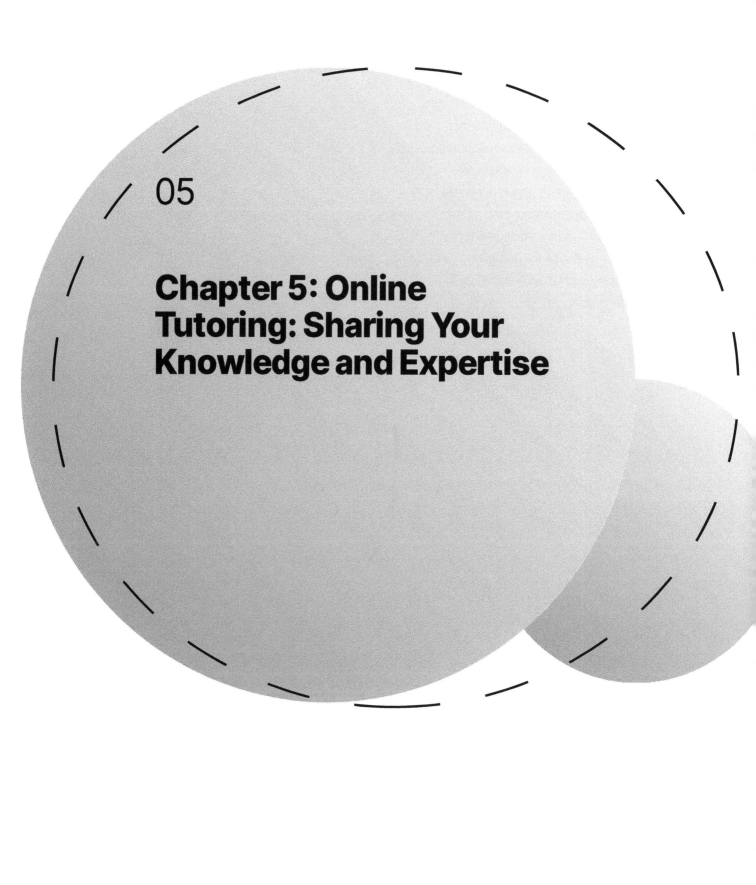

05

Chapter 5: Online Tutoring: Sharing Your Knowledge and Expertise

Introduction to Online Tutoring

In today's digital age, the opportunities for making money online are endless. One such avenue that has gained immense popularity is online tutoring. Whether you are an expert in a particular subject or possess valuable skills that others are eager to learn, online tutoring can be a lucrative way to earn income while helping others achieve their educational goals.

Online tutoring offers a convenient and flexible way for students to access personalized learning from the comfort of their own homes. With just a computer and an internet connection, tutors can connect with students from around the world, transcending geographical boundaries and time zones. This accessibility opens up a vast market of potential clients, making online tutoring a highly scalable business opportunity.

For those with a passion for teaching and a desire to share their knowledge, online tutoring allows you to leverage your expertise and make a significant impact in the lives of others. Whether you are well-versed in academic subjects like math, science, or languages, or possess specialized skills such as music, art, or coding, there is a demand for your expertise in the online tutoring market.

One of the key advantages of online tutoring is the ability to set your own schedule and work at your own pace. As an online tutor, you have the flexibility to choose the hours and days that work best for you, allowing you to strike a balance between your personal and professional commitments. This level of flexibility is especially appealing for those looking to earn extra income alongside their existing jobs or commitments.

To succeed as an online tutor, it is crucial to develop effective communication and teaching techniques. While traditional face-to-face tutoring relies heavily on physical presence and body language, online tutoring requires tutors to adapt their teaching methods to the virtual environment. Utilizing video conferencing platforms, interactive whiteboards, and screen sharing tools, tutors can create an engaging and interactive learning experience for their students.

In the following chapters, we will delve deeper into the world of online tutoring, exploring strategies for marketing your services, building a strong client base, and delivering high-quality lessons. We will also discuss the various platforms and tools available to enhance your tutoring experience and streamline your administrative tasks.

Whether you are a seasoned educator looking to transition into the online realm or an individual with a passion for sharing knowledge, online tutoring offers ample opportunities to monetize your skills and make a meaningful impact. So, join us on this journey to discover the vast potential of online tutoring and unlock the door to financial success while empowering others through education.

Identifying Your Subject and Target Audience

In the vast and ever-expanding world of online money-making opportunities, it is essential to identify your subject and target audience before diving into any venture. Understanding your niche and the people you aim to serve is crucial for success in the online realm. In this subchapter, we will explore the importance of subject identification and how to effectively define your target audience.

When it comes to making money online, there is a plethora of options available. From affiliate marketing and freelancing to dropshipping and online tutoring, the possibilities seem endless. However, to truly excel in any of these areas, you must first identify your subject or niche. This requires introspection, research, and a deep understanding of your own interests, skills, and passions.

Consider the niches mentioned earlier: making money online, affiliate marketing, freelancing, dropshipping, online tutoring, social media management, blogging and content creation, online surveys and market research, virtual assistant services, selling digital products or courses, and e-commerce and online store management. Which of these aligns with your expertise and interests? Which one excites you the most? Identifying your subject is crucial as it will determine your focus and the path you choose to embark on.

Once you have identified your subject, the next step is to define your target audience. Who are the people you aim to serve, and how can you best cater to their needs? Understanding your target audience is essential for effective marketing, content creation, and building a loyal customer base. Conduct thorough market research to identify your audience's demographics, interests, pain points, and desires. This will enable you to tailor your services or products to meet their specific needs and stand out from the competition.

Furthermore, understanding your target audience will help you craft compelling and engaging content that resonates with them. Whether you choose to blog, create online courses, manage social media accounts, or provide virtual assistant services, knowing your audience will allow you to deliver value and establish yourself as an authority in your field.

In conclusion, identifying your subject and target audience is a crucial step in your journey towards becoming an online money maker. By understanding your niche and the people you aim to serve, you will be better equipped to carve a successful path in the vast online landscape. So take the time to reflect on your interests and conduct thorough market research – it will set the foundation for your online money-making endeavors.

Creating Engaging Online Tutoring Sessions

In today's digital age, online tutoring has become a popular way to share knowledge and make money online. With the convenience of technology, both tutors and learners can connect from anywhere in the world, breaking down geographical barriers. However, with the increasing popularity of online tutoring, it is crucial to create engaging and effective online sessions to stand out from the competition and provide value to your learners.

To create engaging online tutoring sessions, it is important to prioritize the learner's needs and preferences. Begin by understanding your target audience's learning style and tailor your sessions accordingly. Some learners may prefer visual aids, while others may respond better to auditory explanations. By incorporating various teaching techniques such as videos, images, and interactive quizzes, you can keep your learners engaged and enhance their understanding of the subject matter. Utilize technology to your advantage. There are numerous online tools and platforms available that can make your tutoring sessions more interactive and collaborative. Consider using virtual whiteboards, screen sharing, and chat features to encourage active participation from your learners. Additionally, use applications that allow you to record your sessions so that your learners can revisit the material at their convenience.

Create a structured and organized curriculum for your online tutoring sessions. Break down complex topics into smaller, digestible chunks and provide clear learning objectives for each session. This will help your learners stay focused and motivated throughout the session. Additionally, create a timetable or schedule for your sessions to ensure a consistent and reliable learning experience for your learners. Engage your learners by encouraging active participation. Ask questions, provide opportunities for discussions, and assign interactive activities to reinforce learning. By involving your learners in the learning process, you not only keep them engaged but also foster a deeper understanding of the subject matter.

Lastly, provide personalized feedback and support to your learners. Regularly assess their progress and provide constructive feedback to help them improve. This personalized attention will make your learners feel valued and motivated to continue their learning journey with you.

In conclusion, creating engaging online tutoring sessions requires careful planning and consideration of your learners' needs. By utilizing technology, creating structured curriculums, encouraging active participation, and providing personalized feedback, you can create a rewarding and effective online tutoring experience for both you and your learners.

Marketing and Growing Your Online Tutoring Business

In today's digital age, the online tutoring industry has seen exponential growth. With the convenience and accessibility of the internet, more and more people are turning to online platforms for their educational needs. If you have a passion for teaching and want to capitalize on this booming market, starting your own online tutoring business can be a lucrative venture. In this subchapter, we will explore effective strategies to market and grow your online tutoring business.

1. Identify Your Target Audience: Before diving into marketing your online tutoring business, it is crucial to identify your target audience. Are you focusing on school students, college applicants, or professionals seeking to enhance their skills? Understanding your target audience will help tailor your marketing efforts and deliver the right message to attract potential clients.

2. Build a Professional Website: A well-designed and user-friendly website is essential for establishing credibility and attracting potential clients. Your website should include information about your tutoring services, testimonials from satisfied students, and a clear call-to-action prompting visitors to contact you.

3. Leverage Social Media: Social media platforms provide a vast opportunity to connect with your target audience. Create engaging content related to educational topics, share success stories of your students, and offer valuable tips and advice. Engage with your followers and build a community around your brand.

4. Collaborate with Influencers: Partnering with influencers in the education space can significantly boost your online presence. Reach out to influential bloggers, YouTube personalities, or educational websites to collaborate on content or promotions. Their endorsement can bring in a stream of potential clients.

5. Offer Free Resources: Providing free resources, such as study guides, practice quizzes, or educational videos, can showcase your expertise and attract students to your tutoring services. Collect email addresses in exchange for these resources to build a mailing list for future marketing campaigns.

6. Utilize SEO Strategies: Optimize your website and content with relevant keywords to improve your search engine rankings. This will increase your visibility and drive organic traffic to your website.

7. Seek Testimonials and Reviews: Positive reviews and testimonials from satisfied students can be a powerful marketing tool. Encourage your students to leave reviews on your website or popular review platforms to build trust and credibility.

8. Network with Schools and Educational Institutions: Reach out to local schools, colleges, and educational institutions to form partnerships or offer your tutoring services as an additional resource. Building relationships with academic institutions can lead to a steady stream of students.

By implementing these marketing strategies, you can effectively promote and grow your online tutoring business. Remember to continuously assess and refine your marketing efforts to adapt to the ever-changing online landscape. With dedication and persistence, your online tutoring business can thrive in the competitive online education market.

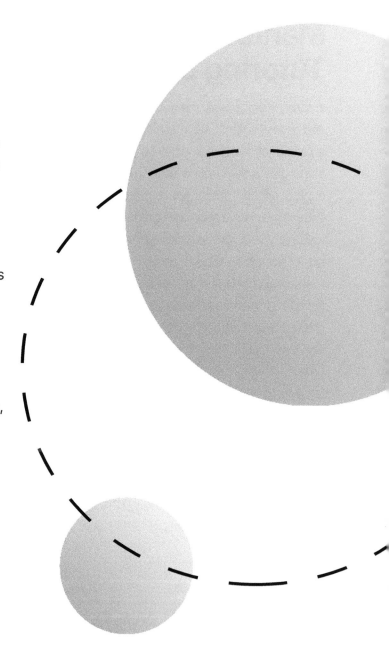

Chapter 6: Social Media Management: Growing an Online Presence

Introduction to Social Media Management

In today's digital age, social media has become an integral part of our lives. It has revolutionized the way we connect, communicate, and consume information. But did you know that social media platforms can also be powerful tools for making money online? Welcome to the world of social media management.

In this subchapter, we will delve into the fundamentals of social media management and how it can be a lucrative avenue for individuals looking to make money online. Whether you are a seasoned entrepreneur or someone exploring new income streams, understanding the ins and outs of social media management can open up a world of opportunities.

Social media management involves creating, planning, and executing strategies to promote brands, businesses, products, or services on various social media platforms. It requires a deep understanding of the target audience, content creation, engagement tactics, and data analysis. As a social media manager, you will play a crucial role in building and maintaining a brand's online presence, increasing its reach, and ultimately driving conversions.

In this subchapter, we will cover the essential aspects of social media management. We will explore the different social media platforms and their unique features, helping you identify the ones that align with your niche and target audience. We will delve into content creation strategies, including creating engaging posts, captivating visuals, and compelling copy. Furthermore, we will discuss the importance of analytics and data-driven decision making in social media management. You will learn how to track and analyze key performance indicators (KPIs) to measure the effectiveness of your strategies and make necessary adjustments to optimize results.

Additionally, we will explore the various monetization methods within social media management. From sponsored posts and affiliate marketing to influencer collaborations and brand partnerships, we will guide you through the process of leveraging your social media presence to generate income.

Whether you aspire to become a social media manager for clients or establish your own online brand, this subchapter will equip you with the knowledge and tools to succeed. So, join us as we embark on an exciting journey into the world of social media management and discover how you can turn your passion for social media into a profitable venture.

Choosing the Right Social Media Platforms

In today's digital age, social media has become an integral part of our daily lives. Not only is it a platform for connecting with friends and family, but it has also opened up endless opportunities for individuals to make money online. However, with numerous social media platforms available, it can be overwhelming to decide which ones are best suited for your online money-making ventures. In this subchapter, we will explore the various factors to consider when choosing the right social media platforms for your specific niche.

When selecting social media platforms, it is crucial to understand your target audience and their preferences. Are they active on Facebook, Instagram, Twitter, or LinkedIn? Conduct market research to identify the platforms where your audience spends the most time and engages with content related to your niche.

Additionally, each social media platform offers unique features and benefits. For instance, if you are in the field of coaching or personal development, platforms like LinkedIn and Facebook groups can be great options to connect with professionals and potential clients. On the other hand, if you are into visual content creation, Instagram and Pinterest can help showcase your work effectively.

Another factor to consider is the type of content you will be creating. If you plan to share informative blog posts or create video tutorials, platforms like YouTube or your own blog would be ideal. However, if you prefer short, snappy content, platforms like Twitter or TikTok may be more suitable.

Furthermore, evaluate the advertising and monetization options available on each platform. Some platforms offer robust advertising tools and the ability to sell products directly, such as Facebook and Instagram. Others, like YouTube, allow you to monetize your content through ads or sponsorships. Understanding these options can help you maximize your earning potential.

Lastly, consider your capacity to manage multiple social media accounts. While it is beneficial to have a presence on various platforms, it is essential to ensure that you can consistently create and engage with content on each one. It is better to excel on a few platforms than to spread yourself too thin across many.

In conclusion, choosing the right social media platforms for your online money-making ventures requires careful consideration. Understanding your target audience, content type, advertising options, and your own capacity will help you make informed decisions. Remember, building a strong presence on social media takes time and effort, so choose platforms that align with your goals and interests to ensure long-term success in your online money-making journey.

Creating Engaging Content and Building a Community

In the digital age, creating engaging content and building a community are essential strategies for anyone looking to make money online. Whether you are a coach, a freelancer, an e-commerce entrepreneur, or a blogger, the ability to capture your audience's attention and connect with them on a deeper level is crucial for success. This subchapter will explore effective techniques for creating engaging content and building a loyal community of followers.

One of the first steps in creating engaging content is understanding your target audience. Take the time to research and analyze the needs, preferences, and pain points of your audience. This will allow you to tailor your content to their specific interests and provide them with valuable solutions. By addressing their needs, you will establish yourself as an authority in your niche and build trust with your audience.

Another important aspect of creating engaging content is storytelling. People are naturally drawn to stories, so incorporating narratives into your content can captivate your audience and make your message more relatable. Share personal experiences, success stories, and case studies that demonstrate the effectiveness of your products or services. This will not only engage your audience but also create an emotional connection that fosters loyalty.

Building a community around your content is equally important. Encourage your audience to interact with your content by asking questions, conducting polls, and requesting feedback. Engage in conversations with your followers and respond to their comments and messages promptly. By creating a sense of community, you will foster a loyal following who will not only consume your content but also share it with others.

Utilizing social media platforms is another powerful tool for building a community. Identify the social media platforms that are most relevant to your target audience and create engaging content specifically for those platforms. Use hashtags, join relevant groups, and collaborate with influencers to expand your reach and attract new followers.

Lastly, consistency is key. Regularly produce high-quality content that is valuable and relevant to your audience. Whether it's through blog posts, videos, podcasts, or social media updates, maintain a consistent schedule to keep your audience engaged and coming back for more.

By implementing these strategies, you can create engaging content and build a community of loyal followers who will not only support your online money-making endeavors but also become your biggest advocates. Remember, building a community takes time and effort, but the rewards are well worth it in the long run.

Analyzing and Optimizing Social Media Strategies

In today's digital age, social media has become an integral part of our lives. It is not only a platform for connecting with friends and sharing personal updates but also a powerful tool for businesses to reach their target audience and promote their products or services. However, just having a presence on social media is not enough. To truly leverage the power of these platforms, it is essential to analyze and optimize your social media strategies.

Analyzing your social media strategies involves examining the data and metrics associated with your social media accounts. This data can provide valuable insights into the effectiveness of your current strategies and help you identify areas for improvement. By analyzing metrics such as engagement rate, reach, and conversions, you can gain a deep understanding of your audience's preferences and behavior. This knowledge will enable you to tailor your content and messaging to better resonate with your target market.

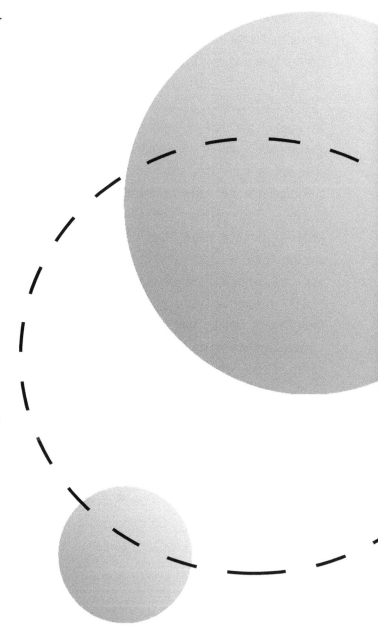

Optimizing your social media strategies involves making adjustments and refinements based on the insights gained from the analysis. This could include experimenting with different content formats, posting schedules, or targeting strategies. By constantly testing and tweaking your social media strategies, you can ensure that you are maximizing your reach and engagement while minimizing wasted resources.

For those in the coaching, money, personal development, finance, and business niches, analyzing and optimizing social media strategies is crucial for success. Whether you are making money online through affiliate marketing, freelancing, dropshipping, online tutoring, or any other online business model, social media can be a game-changer. By effectively utilizing social media platforms, you can attract more clients, increase sales, and establish yourself as an authority in your niche. In this subchapter, we will delve into the specific strategies and techniques that can help you analyze and optimize your social media efforts. From understanding the algorithms of different platforms to utilizing analytics tools and implementing growth hacking tactics, we will provide you with a comprehensive guide to making the most out of social media.

Whether you are a social media manager, a blogger, or an entrepreneur running an online store, this subchapter will equip you with the knowledge and skills to take your social media strategies to the next level. Get ready to unlock the full potential of social media and propel your online business to new heights.

07

Chapter 7: Blogging and Content Creation: Building a Profitable Online Platform

Introduction to Blogging and Content Creation

In today's digital age, the opportunity to make money online has never been more accessible. With the rise of the internet, individuals from all walks of life have found innovative ways to generate income from the comfort of their own homes. One such avenue is through blogging and content creation.

Blogging has become a popular means of expressing oneself, sharing knowledge, and connecting with like-minded individuals. It allows individuals to create their own online platform where they can showcase their expertise, interests, and passions. Whether you're an aspiring writer, a subject matter expert, or simply have a story to tell, blogging provides a unique opportunity to share your voice with the world. Content creation, on the other hand, goes hand in hand with blogging. It involves the creation of engaging and valuable content, such as articles, videos, podcasts, or infographics, that resonates with your target audience. By consistently producing high-quality content, you can attract a loyal following, establish yourself as an authority in your niche, and ultimately monetize your efforts.

For those interested in making money online, blogging and content creation offer numerous avenues for monetization. One of the most common methods is through affiliate marketing, where bloggers promote products or services and earn a commission for every purchase made through their referral links. Freelancing is another option, where bloggers can offer their writing or content creation services to businesses or individuals in need.

Additionally, bloggers can explore dropshipping, online tutoring, social media management, online surveys and market research, virtual assistant services, selling digital products or courses, and even e-commerce and online store management. The opportunities are vast, and with the right strategies and dedication, one can turn their blog into a profitable online business.

In this book, "The Online Money Maker: A Comprehensive Guide to Making Money Online," we will delve into the world of blogging and content creation, providing you with essential tips, strategies, and insights to help you succeed in this exciting field. We will cover topics such as finding your niche, creating engaging content, building and growing your audience, search engine optimization, monetization strategies, and much more.

Whether you're looking to generate a side income, replace your full-time job, or simply pursue your passion for writing and content creation, this book is your roadmap to success. Get ready to embark on a journey that will transform your online presence and financial future. Let's dive into the world of blogging and content creation and unleash your potential as an online money maker.

Selecting a Profitable Blogging Niche

When it comes to making money online, blogging is a popular and potentially lucrative avenue. However, with so many niches to choose from, it can be overwhelming to decide which one will be the most profitable for you. In this subchapter, we will explore the process of selecting a profitable blogging niche that aligns with your interests and goals.

One of the key factors to consider when selecting a niche is your passion and knowledge in a particular area. It is crucial to choose a niche that you are genuinely interested in and can consistently create valuable content about. This will not only make blogging more enjoyable for you, but it will also position you as an authority in your niche, attracting a loyal audience.

Another important aspect to consider is the market demand for your chosen niche. While it is essential to follow your passion, it is equally important to ensure that there is a target audience willing to consume the content you create. Conduct thorough market research to determine if there is a demand for your chosen niche, and identify any gaps or opportunities that you can capitalize on.

Furthermore, consider the profitability of your chosen niche. Some niches naturally lend themselves to more monetization options than others. For example, niches like affiliate marketing, e-commerce, and selling digital products or courses tend to have higher profit potential due to their ability to generate passive income. On the other hand, niches like online surveys and market research may offer lower profitability but can still be a valuable addition to your overall blogging strategy.

It is important to note that selecting a niche is not a one-time decision. As you delve deeper into your blogging journey, you may discover new interests, trends may change, or market demands may shift. Therefore, it is crucial to stay flexible and adapt your niche as needed to ensure long-term profitability. In conclusion, selecting a profitable blogging niche requires a balance between your passion, market demand, and profitability. By choosing a niche that you are genuinely interested in, that has a target audience willing to consume your content, and that offers potential for monetization, you will be on your way to becoming a successful online money maker.

Creating Valuable and Engaging Content

In today's digital landscape, the key to success in any online venture lies in creating valuable and engaging content. Whether you are a blogger, a social media manager, or an online tutor, the quality of your content will determine the level of success you achieve. This subchapter will provide you with practical tips and strategies to create content that captivates your audience and drives results.

To start with, it is crucial to understand the needs and interests of your target audience. Take the time to conduct market research and identify what topics resonate with them the most. By addressing their pain points, providing solutions, and delivering information that they find valuable, you will establish yourself as an authority in your niche.

One effective approach to creating valuable content is to share your personal experiences and insights. People are often drawn to authentic stories that they can relate to. By sharing your own journey and the lessons you've learned along the way, you will establish a genuine connection with your audience and gain their trust.

Additionally, make sure to incorporate a variety of media formats in your content. This could include written articles, videos, infographics, podcasts, and more. Different people consume information in different ways, so by diversifying your content, you can cater to a wider audience and keep them engaged.

Furthermore, always strive to make your content visually appealing and easy to read. Use eye-catching headlines, subheadings, and bullet points to break up the text and make it more scannable. Incorporate relevant images, charts, and graphs to provide visual support to your message.

Lastly, don't forget to interact with your audience. Engage with comments on your blog, social media platforms, or online courses. Respond to their questions, address their concerns, and show genuine interest in their feedback. This will not only help you build a loyal community but also give you valuable insights into what your audience wants to see more of.

In conclusion, creating valuable and engaging content is the backbone of any successful online venture. By understanding your target audience, sharing personal experiences, utilizing different media formats, and interacting with your audience, you will be able to create content that captivates and drives results. So, go ahead and apply these strategies to your online business and watch as your audience grows and your profits soar.

Monetizing Your Blog and Growing Your Audience

In today's digital age, the potential to make money online is immense. One of the most popular and effective ways to achieve this is by starting a blog. Whether you are passionate about coaching, money, personal development, finance, or business, blogging can be a lucrative venture that allows you to share your expertise and connect with a wide audience. This subchapter of "The Online Money Maker: A Comprehensive Guide to Making Money Online" is dedicated to helping you monetize your blog and grow your audience in order to maximize your online income.

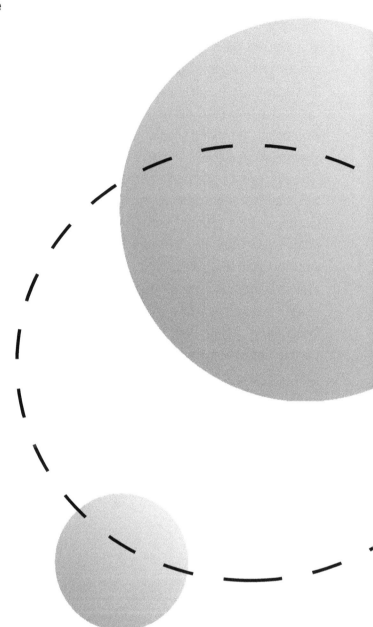

First and foremost, it is crucial to create valuable and engaging content that resonates with your target audience. By consistently providing high-quality articles, tutorials, or thought-provoking insights, you can build a loyal readership base. This will not only increase your credibility but also attract potential advertisers and sponsors. Affiliate marketing is a particularly effective strategy for bloggers. By promoting products or services related to your niche and including affiliate links, you can earn a commission for every sale made through your blog.

Freelancing is another avenue that can bring in additional income through your blog. Utilize your expertise and offer your services to your readers as a freelancer in your field. Whether it's writing, graphic design, or web development, your blog can serve as a portfolio and showcase your skills to potential clients.

Additionally, consider incorporating dropshipping into your blog. This e-commerce model allows you to sell products without the need for inventory or shipping. By partnering with suppliers, you can set up an online store and promote products relevant to your niche. This way, you can earn a profit from each sale made through your blog.

Furthermore, online tutoring and social media management are growing industries that can be integrated into your blog to generate income. If you have expertise in a particular subject, offer online tutoring services to your readers. Alternatively, leverage your social media skills and manage social media accounts for individuals or businesses seeking to expand their online presence.

By conducting online surveys and market research, you can also earn money while gaining insights into your audience's preferences and needs. Furthermore, consider offering virtual assistant services to busy professionals or entrepreneurs who require help with administrative tasks.

Selling digital products or courses is another effective way to monetize your blog. Create and sell e-books, online courses, or other digital products that provide value to your readers. This allows you to leverage your expertise and offer additional resources to your audience.

Lastly, if you have a knack for e-commerce and online store management, consider setting up an online store on your blog. This way, you can sell physical products directly to your audience and earn a profit from each sale.

In conclusion, monetizing your blog and growing your audience is an essential aspect of making money online. By implementing strategies such as affiliate marketing, freelancing, dropshipping, online tutoring, social media management, blogging and content creation, online surveys and market research, virtual assistant services, selling digital products or courses, and e-commerce and online store management, you can maximize your online income and create a sustainable online business.

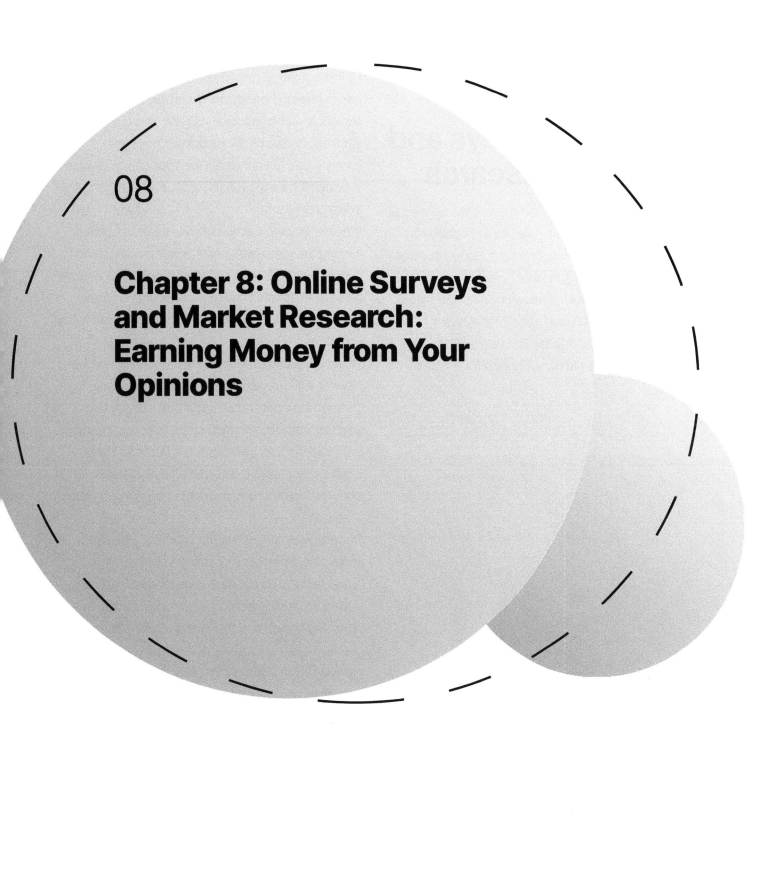

08

Chapter 8: Online Surveys and Market Research: Earning Money from Your Opinions

Introduction to Online Surveys and Market Research

In today's digital age, the internet has opened up a plethora of opportunities for individuals to make money online. One such avenue that has gained popularity in recent years is online surveys and market research. This subchapter will provide you with a comprehensive introduction to this exciting field and how you can leverage it to generate income.

Online surveys and market research play a crucial role in helping businesses understand their target audience, gather valuable insights, and make informed decisions. By participating in these surveys, you not only have the opportunity to voice your opinions and preferences but also earn money in the process.

Whether you are a stay-at-home parent, a student looking for some extra cash, or someone looking to supplement their existing income, online surveys can be a viable option. They require minimal time and effort, making them suitable for individuals with busy schedules.

To get started with online surveys, you will need to register with reputable survey platforms. These platforms connect businesses with individuals like yourself, who are willing to share their opinions in exchange for compensation. It is important to choose reliable platforms that offer legitimate opportunities and ensure your personal information is secure.

Once registered, you will start receiving survey invitations based on your demographic profile. These surveys can cover a wide range of topics, from consumer preferences to market trends. By providing honest and thoughtful responses, you contribute to the accuracy of the data collected and increase your chances of receiving more survey opportunities.

In addition to surveys, market research companies may also offer other opportunities such as product testing, focus groups, or online discussions. These activities allow you to delve deeper into specific topics and provide more detailed feedback.

While online surveys can be a great way to make money, it is essential to set realistic expectations. The compensation for each survey may vary, ranging from a few cents to a few dollars. However, with consistent participation and by signing up with multiple survey platforms, you can maximize your earning potential.

In conclusion, online surveys and market research offer an accessible and flexible way to earn money online. By sharing your opinions and insights, you can not only contribute to the growth of businesses but also generate income for yourself. So, get ready to share your thoughts, make money, and embark on an exciting journey in the world of online surveys and market research.

Finding Legitimate Survey Sites and Research Opportunities

In the digital age, making money online has become a popular choice for individuals seeking financial independence and flexibility. One of the most accessible avenues to earn extra income is by participating in online surveys and research opportunities. However, the internet is filled with scams and fraudulent websites that promise easy money, making it crucial to find legitimate survey sites and research opportunities.

To ensure your time and effort are well-spent, it is important to follow a few guidelines when searching for reputable platforms. Firstly, always do thorough research before signing up or sharing any personal information. Look for reviews and testimonials from other users to gauge the platform's credibility and legitimacy. Reputable survey sites and research opportunities often have a positive track record and are transparent about their payment terms and procedures.

Additionally, it is advisable to stick to well-known survey sites and research panels. These platforms have established themselves in the industry and are more likely to offer legitimate opportunities. Look out for trustworthy names such as Swagbucks, Survey Junkie, or Vindale Research, which have been around for years and have a large user base. Such platforms often provide regular surveys and research opportunities, ensuring a steady stream of income.

Furthermore, consider joining online communities and forums dedicated to making money online. These communities can provide valuable insights and recommendations on legitimate survey sites and research opportunities. Members often share their experiences and discuss the best platforms to join, helping you avoid scams and maximize your earning potential.

It is essential to be realistic about the income potential of online surveys and research. While they can provide a valuable source of supplemental income, they are unlikely to replace a full-time job. Treat survey sites and research opportunities as a way to earn extra cash or gift cards rather than a primary income source.

In conclusion, finding legitimate survey sites and research opportunities requires diligence and caution in the online space. Research thoroughly, stick to well-known platforms, and seek advice from online communities to ensure you are participating in reputable opportunities. By following these guidelines, you can make the most of your time and effort, earning extra income while avoiding scams and fraudulent websites.

Maximizing Your Earnings from Online Surveys

In today's digital age, there are numerous ways to make money online. One of the increasingly popular methods is by participating in online surveys. Companies and organizations are constantly seeking valuable consumer insights, and they are willing to pay for your opinions. However, if you want to maximize your earnings from online surveys, there are a few strategies that you should keep in mind.

First and foremost, it's essential to sign up for reputable survey sites. There are countless options available, but not all of them are legitimate or worth your time. Do your research and choose platforms that have a proven track record of delivering surveys and compensating participants promptly. Look for reviews and testimonials from other users to ensure that you are dealing with a trustworthy site.

Once you have selected the right survey sites, it's crucial to complete your profile accurately and honestly. Many surveys are targeted towards specific demographic groups, and by providing accurate information about yourself, you increase your chances of receiving more survey invitations. Moreover, some sites offer monetary bonuses for completing your profile, so take advantage of these opportunities.

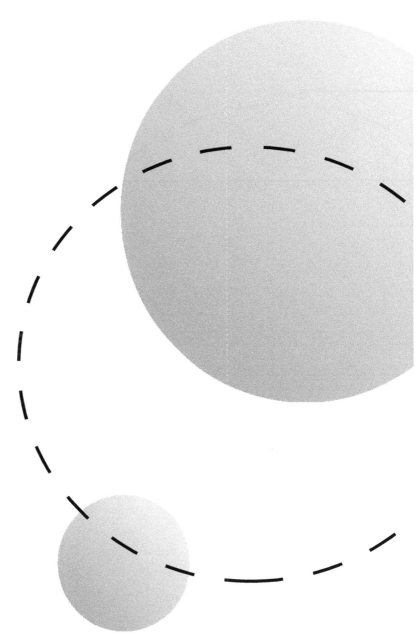

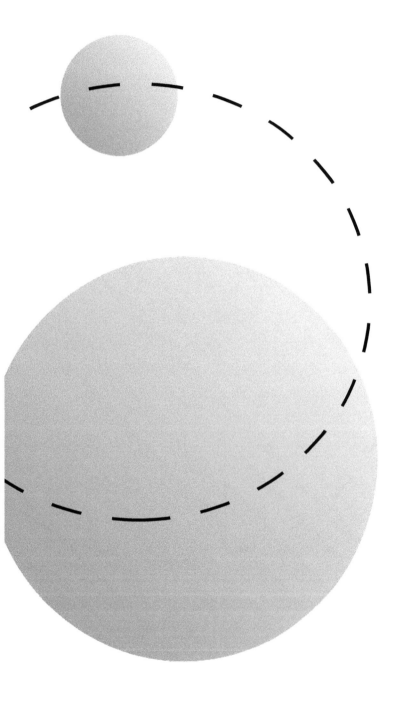

Another way to maximize your earnings is by being proactive. Instead of waiting for survey invitations to come to you, check the survey sites regularly for available surveys. Many surveys have limited spots, and by being one of the first to participate, you increase your chances of qualifying and earning money. Additionally, consider joining multiple survey sites to diversify your income streams. Different sites offer different survey opportunities, and by spreading your efforts across multiple platforms, you increase your chances of finding surveys that match your interests and demographics. This can significantly boost your earnings.

Furthermore, staying engaged with the survey community can also be beneficial. Participate in forums or online communities where survey takers share tips and information about high-paying surveys. By networking with other survey takers, you can discover new opportunities and learn from their experiences. Lastly, be patient and persistent. Online surveys may not make you rich overnight, but with consistent effort, you can steadily increase your earnings. Treat survey taking as a part-time job and allocate dedicated time each day or week to complete surveys. The more surveys you complete, the more money you can make.

In conclusion, online surveys can be a lucrative way to make money from the comfort of your own home. By following these strategies and putting in consistent effort, you can maximize your earnings and make the most out of this online money-making opportunity.

Leveraging Market Research Skills for Higher Paying Opportunities

In today's digital age, the opportunities to make money online are vast and varied. Whether you're an aspiring entrepreneur, a freelancer, or someone looking to boost their income, the online world offers a multitude of avenues to explore. However, to truly succeed and maximize your earnings, it's essential to develop market research skills that can help you identify higher paying opportunities.

Market research is the foundation of any successful business venture. By understanding your target audience, their needs, preferences, and buying behaviors, you can tailor your products or services to meet their demands effectively. This principle applies to online money-making opportunities as well. By leveraging your market research skills, you can position yourself in the most profitable niches and attract higher-paying clients or customers.

One of the first steps to leveraging market research skills is to identify the niches that offer the most lucrative opportunities. This could involve conducting comprehensive keyword research to uncover high-demand and low-competition keywords related to your chosen field. For example, if you're interested in affiliate marketing, you might use keyword research tools to find profitable niches within the broader realm of affiliate marketing, such as "best affiliate programs for online courses" or "top affiliate programs for health supplements."

Once you've identified the niches, your market research skills can help you better understand your target audience. By conducting surveys, analyzing social media trends, and studying competitor strategies, you can gain valuable insights into what your audience wants and needs. This information can then be used to create compelling content, develop products or services, or refine your marketing strategies to attract higher-paying opportunities.

Furthermore, market research skills can also be utilized to analyze and evaluate potential clients or customers. When freelancing or offering virtual assistant services, for example, you might conduct research on clients' businesses, their target markets, and their competitors. This knowledge can help you showcase your expertise and demonstrate how you can add value to their operations, leading to higher-paying contracts.

In conclusion, market research skills are invaluable for anyone looking to make money online. By leveraging these skills, you can identify the most lucrative niches, understand your target audience better, and attract higher-paying opportunities. Whether you're interested in affiliate marketing, freelancing, dropshipping, or any other online money-making venture, investing time and effort into honing your market research skills will undoubtedly pay off in the long run. So, don't overlook the power of market research and seize the higher-paying opportunities that await you in the vast online marketplace.

09

Chapter 9: Virtual Assistant Services: Providing Remote Administrative Support

Introduction to Virtual Assistant Services

In today's fast-paced digital world, the demand for virtual assistant services has skyrocketed. As businesses and individuals strive to stay ahead of the competition and manage their time effectively, virtual assistants have become indispensable. This subchapter will provide you with a comprehensive introduction to virtual assistant services, shedding light on how this niche can help you make money online.

Virtual assistant services encompass a wide range of tasks that can be performed remotely. From administrative support to social media management, online surveys to e-commerce management, a virtual assistant can handle various responsibilities based on the needs of their clients. This flexibility makes it an ideal field for individuals looking to make money online.

One of the most popular virtual assistant services is social media management. With the increasing influence of social media platforms, businesses and individuals are constantly seeking professionals who can handle their online presence. As a virtual assistant, you can create engaging content, schedule posts, and interact with followers, helping businesses build a strong online presence and increase their reach.

Another lucrative area within virtual assistant services is e-commerce and online store management. With the rise of online shopping, businesses are always on the lookout for virtual assistants who can handle their online stores, manage inventory, process orders, and provide customer support. This niche offers great potential for making money online, especially for individuals with a flair for organization and customer service.

Virtual assistants can also specialize in blogging and content creation. As more individuals and businesses turn to blogging as a means of communication and marketing, there is a growing demand for skilled writers who can create engaging and informative content. By offering your services as a virtual assistant in this niche, you can assist clients in creating blog posts, articles, and other written content that drives traffic and boosts their online presence.

Whether you have experience in administrative tasks, social media management, or content creation, becoming a virtual assistant can be a lucrative opportunity to make money online. By specializing in different niches such as affiliate marketing, freelancing, dropshipping, online tutoring, or selling digital products, you can cater to a specific audience and carve out a profitable niche for yourself.
In the following chapters, we will delve deeper into the various aspects of virtual assistant services, providing you with practical tips, strategies, and resources to kickstart your journey as a successful virtual assistant. Prepare to explore the exciting world of virtual assistant services, where the possibilities for making money online are endless!

Identifying In-Demand Virtual Assistant Skills

In today's digital age, the demand for virtual assistants is skyrocketing. As more and more individuals and businesses look to outsource their tasks and streamline their operations, the need for skilled virtual assistants continues to grow. If you're interested in entering the world of virtual assistance, it's crucial to understand the in-demand skills that can set you apart from the competition.

1. Organization and Time Management: As a virtual assistant, you'll likely be juggling multiple tasks and projects simultaneously. Being highly organized and skilled in time management is essential to ensure that you meet deadlines and deliver high-quality work.

2. Communication: Effective communication is a key skill for any virtual assistant. Whether it's communicating with clients, team members, or stakeholders, being able to convey information clearly and professionally is crucial. Strong written and verbal communication skills will help you build trust and maintain strong relationships with your clients.

3. Tech Savviness: As a virtual assistant, you'll be working remotely and utilizing various online tools and software. Having a good understanding of technology and being comfortable with different platforms and applications will help you navigate the virtual working environment with ease.

4. Flexibility and Adaptability: The online landscape is constantly evolving, and as a virtual assistant, you'll need to be adaptable to new technologies, trends, and client needs. Being flexible and open to learning new skills will keep you relevant in the ever-changing online world.

5. Problem-solving: Clients often turn to virtual assistants for their problem-solving abilities. Being able to identify issues, think critically, and propose solutions is a valuable skill that will make you an invaluable asset to your clients.

6. Attention to Detail: In the virtual world, accuracy and attention to detail are paramount. Being meticulous in your work, double-checking for errors, and ensuring that all tasks are completed to the highest standard will help you maintain a professional reputation.

7. Social Media Management: With the rise of social media platforms, businesses are increasingly seeking virtual assistants who can help them manage their online presence. Having a good understanding of social media platforms, content creation, and engagement strategies will make you a sought-after virtual assistant in this niche.

By developing and honing these in-demand virtual assistant skills, you'll position yourself as a valuable asset in the online marketplace. Whether you choose to specialize in a specific niche or offer a wide range of services, these skills will help you stand out and thrive in the ever-growing world of virtual assistance.

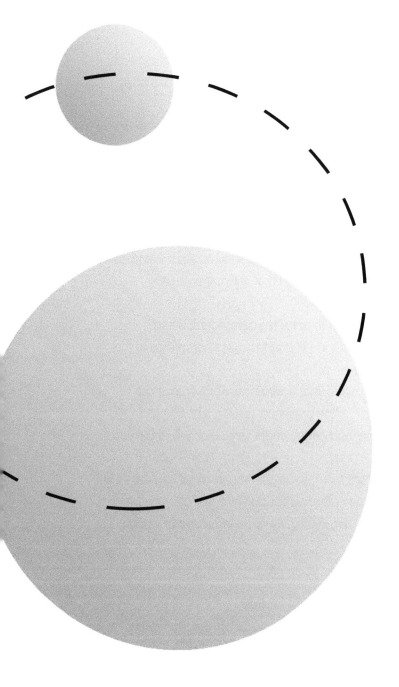

Creating a Professional Virtual Assistant Profile

In today's digital age, virtual assistants have become an integral part of businesses and entrepreneurs looking to streamline their operations. As a virtual assistant, your online profile serves as your virtual business card, showcasing your skills, expertise, and professionalism. In this subchapter, we will delve into the key components of creating a professional virtual assistant profile that will attract clients from various industries.

First and foremost, your profile should highlight your relevant experience and skills. Whether you specialize in social media management, content creation, or administrative tasks, clearly articulate your expertise and provide concrete examples of your past projects. This will instill trust and confidence in potential clients, assuring them that you are capable of delivering high-quality work.

Additionally, it is crucial to showcase your qualifications and certifications. If you have completed any relevant courses or obtained certifications in your field, be sure to mention them in your profile. This not only adds credibility to your profile but also demonstrates your commitment to professional growth and development.

Furthermore, a professional virtual assistant profile should include testimonials and reviews from satisfied clients. Consider reaching out to previous clients or employers and request their feedback on your work. These testimonials act as social proof, validating your skills and abilities, and can significantly increase your chances of securing new clients.

Another essential aspect of your profile is clearly stating your availability and rates. Clients want to know if you are available for ongoing, part-time, or full-time work, as well as your hourly or project-based rates. Being transparent about your availability and rates will help potential clients determine if you are a good fit for their needs and budget.

Lastly, make sure to include a professional headshot and a brief introduction about yourself. Clients want to know who they will be working with, so a friendly and approachable photo can go a long way in building trust and rapport. Additionally, a concise and engaging introduction will provide potential clients with a glimpse into your personality and work ethic.

By following these guidelines and creating a professional virtual assistant profile, you will position yourself as a highly sought-after professional in the world of online business. Remember to regularly update your profile with new skills, certifications, and testimonials to stay competitive in this ever-evolving field.

Finding and Retaining Virtual Assistant Clients

As a virtual assistant, finding and retaining clients is essential for your success in the online business world. Whether you offer social media management, online tutoring, or e-commerce and online store management services, the strategies outlined in this subchapter will help you attract and keep clients.

1. Define your ideal client: Before you start searching for clients, it's crucial to identify your target audience. Determine the type of clients you want to work with based on your skills, interests, and niche. This will help you tailor your marketing efforts to attract the right clients.

2. Build an online presence: In today's digital age, having a strong online presence is vital. Create a professional website and optimize it for search engines. Use social media platforms to showcase your expertise and engage with potential clients. Consider starting a blog or YouTube channel to share valuable content that establishes you as an authority in your field.

3. Network and collaborate: Networking is a powerful tool when it comes to finding clients. Join online communities and forums related to your niche, attend virtual conferences and webinars, and connect with other professionals in your industry. Collaborating with others can also open doors to new client opportunities.

4. Offer a free consultation or trial: To attract potential clients, offer a free consultation or trial of your services. This allows them to experience the value you provide firsthand. During this period, showcase your skills and demonstrate how you can solve their pain points effectively.

5. Provide exceptional customer service: One of the keys to retaining clients is to provide exceptional customer service. Respond promptly to inquiries, be proactive in addressing their needs, and go the extra mile to exceed their expectations. Happy clients are more likely to refer you to others and continue working with you.

6. Offer package deals or discounts: To incentivize clients to work with you long-term, consider offering package deals or discounts. This not only encourages them to commit to a longer-term arrangement but also helps you secure a steady stream of income.

Remember, finding and retaining clients as a virtual assistant requires dedication, persistence, and continuous improvement. By implementing these strategies and adapting them to your specific niche, you can build a thriving online business and achieve financial success.

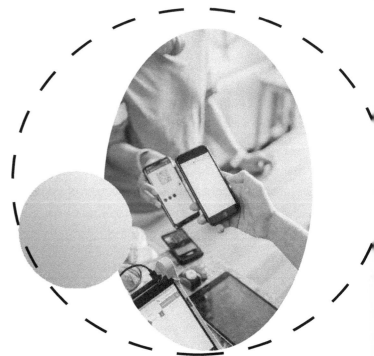

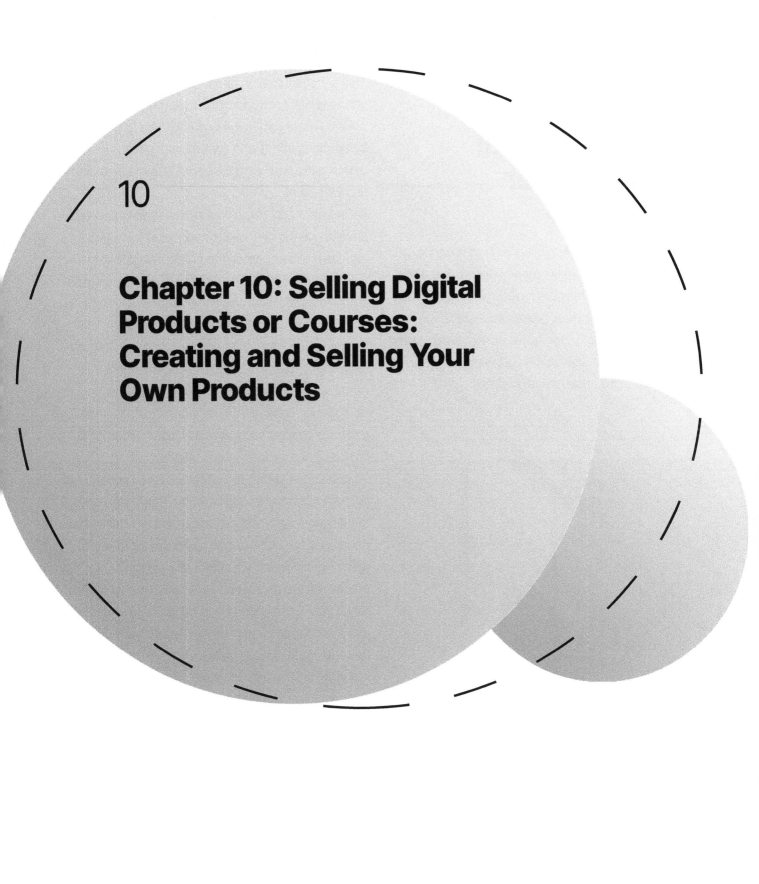

10

Chapter 10: Selling Digital Products or Courses: Creating and Selling Your Own Products

Introduction to Selling Digital Products or Courses

In today's digital age, there is an abundance of opportunities to make money online. One of the most lucrative avenues is selling digital products or courses. Whether you are an expert in a specific field or possess valuable knowledge and skills, you can tap into this growing market and create a profitable online business.

This subchapter aims to provide an introduction to selling digital products or courses, equipping you with the essential knowledge and tools to embark on this exciting venture. We will explore various aspects of this niche, including the benefits, strategies, and tips for success.

Selling digital products or courses offers numerous advantages. Firstly, it allows you to leverage your expertise and knowledge to create valuable content that can help others. This not only provides a sense of fulfillment but also positions you as an authority in your field. Secondly, the online nature of this business eliminates the need for physical inventory, shipping, or storage costs, making it a highly scalable and cost-effective option. Lastly, the potential for passive income is immense, as once you have created and marketed your product or course, it can generate sales on autopilot.

To succeed in selling digital products or courses, it is crucial to develop a solid strategy. This involves identifying your target audience, understanding their needs and pain points, and tailoring your offerings to meet those demands. Additionally, effective marketing and promotion strategies are essential to reach your target market and generate sales. We will delve into these topics further, providing practical tips and techniques to help you stand out in the crowded online marketplace.

Furthermore, we will explore different types of digital products or courses you can create, ranging from e-books, video tutorials, online courses, and membership sites. Each format has its unique advantages and considerations, and we will guide you in choosing the most suitable option based on your expertise and audience.

Selling digital products or courses is a dynamic and ever-evolving field, and staying updated with the latest trends and tools is crucial for success. Throughout this subchapter, we will provide insights into emerging trends, popular platforms, and tools to streamline your business operations.

By the end of this subchapter, you will have a comprehensive understanding of the fundamentals of selling digital products or courses. Whether you are a coach, freelancer, or aspiring entrepreneur, this knowledge will empower you to create a profitable online business and achieve financial independence. So, let's dive in and explore the exciting world of selling digital products or courses!

Identifying Profitable Product or Course Ideas

In the vast world of online money-making opportunities, it can be overwhelming to decide which path to pursue. Whether you're interested in affiliate marketing, freelancing, dropshipping, or any other online venture, the first step toward success is identifying profitable product or course ideas. This subchapter will provide you with valuable insights and strategies to help you narrow down your options and find the most lucrative opportunities in your niche.

One key aspect of identifying profitable ideas is understanding your target audience. Regardless of the niche you choose, it is essential to know your potential customers' needs, desires, and pain points. Conduct thorough market research to gain insights into what products or courses are in high demand. Look for gaps in the market that you can fill with your unique offering.

Another approach is to analyze popular trends and emerging markets. Stay up-to-date with the latest industry news and identify emerging niches that have the potential for growth. For example, if you're interested in social media management, keep an eye out for platforms or strategies that are gaining traction. Being an early adopter in a new and promising niche can give you a significant advantage.

Consider your own expertise and passions. What are you knowledgeable about, and what are you genuinely passionate about? Building a profitable online business requires dedication and long-term commitment. If you choose a niche that aligns with your skills and interests, you'll be more motivated to put in the necessary time and effort.

Once you have a list of potential ideas, it's essential to validate their profitability. Look for indicators such as market demand, competition analysis, and potential profit margins. Conduct surveys, polls, or interviews to gather feedback from your target audience. This will help you fine-tune your product or course idea to meet their specific needs and preferences.

Furthermore, consider the scalability of your chosen idea. Can it be easily expanded or diversified in the future? This is crucial for long-term success and growth. Explore opportunities to create additional products or courses within the same niche, or consider how your idea could be adapted to different markets or platforms.

Identifying profitable product or course ideas is a crucial step toward online success. By understanding your target audience, staying informed about trends, and validating your ideas, you can set yourself up for a profitable online venture. Remember, the key to success lies in finding the perfect balance between your skills, passion, and market demand.

Creating and Packaging Your Digital Products or Courses

In today's digital era, there are countless opportunities to monetize your skills and expertise online. Whether you're a coach, an entrepreneur, or someone with a passion for personal development, creating and packaging your digital products or courses can be a game-changer for your income streams. In this subchapter, we will explore the essential steps and strategies to successfully launch and sell your digital products or courses.

The first step in creating your digital product or course is to identify your target audience and their needs. Understanding who your ideal customer is and what problems they are looking to solve will help you create a product that resonates with them. Conduct market research, engage with your audience through social media or surveys, and gather feedback to ensure you're addressing their pain points effectively.

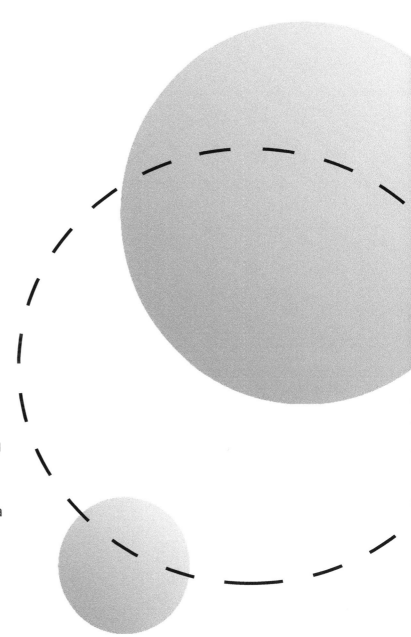

Once you have a clear understanding of your target audience, it's time to create your product or course content. Whether it's an e-book, a video course, or a membership site, ensure that your content is valuable, actionable, and well-structured. Take the time to research and organize your material, and consider using multimedia elements such as videos, infographics, or interactive quizzes to enhance the learning experience.

Packaging your digital product or course is crucial for attracting potential customers. Design an eye-catching cover, write compelling sales copy, and create a landing page that highlights the benefits and features of your product. Use persuasive language to convey the value your product offers and include testimonials or case studies to establish credibility.

Marketing and promoting your digital product or course is essential to drive sales. Leverage your existing online platforms, such as your website, blog, or social media channels, to create buzz and generate interest. Consider partnering with influencers or affiliates in your niche to expand your reach and tap into their audience.

Lastly, ensure that your sales process is seamless and user-friendly. Set up an easy-to-use payment gateway, provide clear instructions on how to access your product, and offer exceptional customer support. Encourage satisfied customers to leave reviews or testimonials, as positive feedback can significantly impact your future sales.

Creating and packaging your digital products or courses can open up a world of opportunities for generating income online. By understanding your audience, creating valuable content, and effectively marketing your product, you can build a sustainable and profitable online business in the coaching, personal development, finance, or business niches. So, take action, unleash your creativity, and start making money online today.

Marketing and Selling Your Digital Products or Courses

In today's digital age, there are countless opportunities to make money online. Whether you are a coach, a freelancer, or an entrepreneur, selling digital products or courses can be a lucrative venture. However, with the increasing competition in the online marketplace, it is essential to have a well-thought-out marketing and sales strategy to stand out from the crowd and maximize your profits. When it comes to marketing your digital products or courses, one of the most effective strategies is to build a strong online presence. This can be done through various channels such as social media, blogging, and content creation. By consistently providing valuable and engaging content related to your niche, you can attract a loyal following who are more likely to purchase your products or enroll in your courses.

Additionally, affiliate marketing can be a powerful tool to reach a wider audience and boost your sales. By partnering with influencers or affiliates who have a large following in your niche, you can leverage their reach and credibility to promote your products or courses. Offering them a commission for every sale they generate can incentivize them to promote your offerings enthusiastically.

Furthermore, utilizing email marketing can help you build a direct relationship with your audience. By offering a freebie or lead magnet in exchange for their email address, you can nurture them through automated email sequences and provide value even before they make a purchase. This builds trust and increases the likelihood of conversion.

In terms of sales, it is crucial to have a user-friendly and visually appealing website or sales page. Clearly articulate the benefits and features of your digital products or courses and include testimonials or case studies to establish credibility. Simplify the purchasing process and offer multiple payment options to cater to different preferences.

Lastly, continuously gathering feedback from your customers and incorporating their suggestions can help you improve your offerings and increase customer satisfaction. Positive reviews and word-of-mouth referrals can significantly boost your sales and reputation.

In conclusion, marketing and selling your digital products or courses requires a comprehensive strategy that includes building an online presence, utilizing affiliate marketing and email marketing, and creating a user-friendly sales process. By implementing these strategies and adapting to the ever-evolving online marketplace, you can maximize your profits and establish yourself as a successful online money maker.

11

Chapter 11: E-commerce and Online Store Management: Running a Profitable Online Store

Introduction to E-commerce and Online Store Management

In today's digital age, the internet has revolutionized the way we do business. The growth of e-commerce has opened up endless opportunities for individuals to make money online. Whether you are a seasoned entrepreneur or a beginner looking to dip your toes into the world of online business, understanding the fundamentals of e-commerce and online store management is crucial.

This subchapter aims to provide you with a comprehensive introduction to e-commerce and equip you with the necessary knowledge to successfully manage an online store. We will explore various aspects of online business, from setting up an e-commerce website to effectively marketing and managing your online store.

Firstly, we will delve into the different types of online business models, such as dropshipping, affiliate marketing, freelancing, and selling digital products or courses. Each model has its unique advantages and challenges, and we will discuss how to choose the right one for your niche and skills.

Next, we will guide you through the process of setting up an e-commerce website. From selecting a domain name and web hosting provider to designing an appealing and user-friendly interface, we will provide you with step-by-step instructions to create a professional online store.

Once your online store is up and running, we will explore various strategies to drive traffic and generate sales. Topics such as search engine optimization (SEO), social media management, blogging and content creation, and online surveys and market research will be covered in detail. By understanding these marketing techniques, you will be able to effectively promote your products or services and reach your target audience.

Furthermore, we will discuss the importance of customer experience and how to provide exceptional customer service. From optimizing your website's checkout process to implementing effective communication channels, we will help you cultivate a loyal customer base and foster repeat business. Lastly, we will touch upon the importance of analytics and data tracking in online store management. By utilizing various tools and software, you will gain insights into customer behavior, sales performance, and marketing strategies. These analytics will enable you to make informed decisions and continuously improve your online store's performance.

Whether you aspire to become a successful e-commerce entrepreneur or simply want to supplement your income through online business, this subchapter will provide you with the necessary knowledge and skills to thrive in the world of e-commerce and online store management. Get ready to embark on an exciting journey of making money online!

Choosing the Right E-commerce Platform

In today's digital age, having an online presence is crucial for anyone looking to make money online. Whether you're a freelancer, an affiliate marketer, or an aspiring entrepreneur, having an e-commerce platform is essential for success. But with so many options available, how do you choose the right one for your specific needs?

When it comes to selecting an e-commerce platform, there are several factors to consider. First and foremost, you need to determine your goals and objectives. Are you looking to sell physical products, digital goods, or services? Understanding your business model will help you narrow down your options.

Next, you need to assess the features and functionality offered by different platforms. Look for features like easy product listing and inventory management, secure payment gateways, customizable themes, and mobile responsiveness. These features will ensure a smooth and seamless shopping experience for your customers.

Another crucial aspect to consider is the scalability of the platform. As your business grows, you'll need a platform that can accommodate your expanding needs. Look for platforms that offer flexible pricing plans and the ability to integrate with other tools and services.

Furthermore, it's important to consider the level of technical expertise required to operate the platform. Some platforms are user-friendly and require no coding knowledge, while others may require more technical skills. Assess your own abilities and choose a platform that aligns with your skillset.

Additionally, it's essential to consider the level of customer support provided by the platform. When you encounter technical issues or have questions, it's crucial to have access to reliable and responsive support. Look for platforms that offer 24/7 support through multiple channels, such as live chat, email, and phone.

Lastly, take into account the cost of the e-commerce platform. While some platforms offer free plans, they often come with limitations. Consider your budget and compare the pricing plans of different platforms to find the best value for your money.

In conclusion, choosing the right e-commerce platform is a critical decision for anyone looking to make money online. By considering factors such as your business goals, features and functionality, scalability, technical expertise required, customer support, and cost, you can make an informed decision that aligns with your specific needs. Remember, your e-commerce platform is the foundation of your online business, so choose wisely and set yourself up for success.

Optimizing Product Listings and Conversions

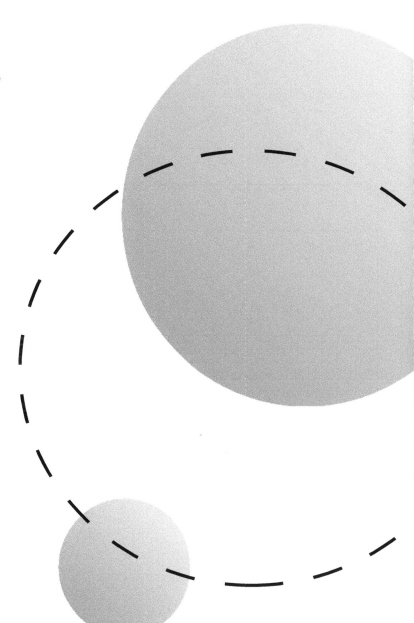

In the ever-evolving world of online business, it is crucial to optimize your product listings and conversions in order to maximize your profits. Whether you are engaged in affiliate marketing, dropshipping, or managing your own e-commerce store, understanding the art of effective product optimization can take your online money-making endeavors to new heights.

When it comes to optimizing product listings, the first step is to conduct thorough market research. By understanding your target audience's needs and desires, you can tailor your product listings to attract their attention and convince them to make a purchase. Take advantage of online surveys and market research tools to gather valuable insights into your customers' preferences and pain points. Next, focus on crafting compelling product descriptions. Your potential customers rely solely on the information you provide to make a purchasing decision. Therefore, it is essential to create descriptions that are not only accurate but also persuasive. Highlight the unique selling points of your products, emphasize their benefits, and address any potential objections or concerns that your audience may have.

In addition to well-written descriptions, high-quality visuals are vital for optimizing product listings. Invest in professional product photography or create visually appealing graphics that showcase your products from different angles and in various contexts. Remember, a picture is worth a thousand words, and eye-catching visuals can significantly impact your conversions. Furthermore, consider incorporating customer testimonials and reviews into your product listings. Social proof plays a crucial role in building trust and credibility with your audience. Positive feedback from satisfied customers can reassure potential buyers and increase their likelihood of making a purchase.

Once your product listings are optimized, it is time to focus on conversion rate optimization (CRO). This involves analyzing your website's user experience, identifying areas of improvement, and implementing changes to enhance conversions. Test different versions of your product pages, experiment with different calls-to-action, and optimize your checkout process to minimize friction and increase conversions.

Remember, optimizing product listings and conversions is an ongoing process. Continuously monitor your analytics, gather customer feedback, and stay updated with industry trends to fine-tune your strategies and drive even more success in your online money-making ventures.

Whether you are a seasoned online entrepreneur or just starting your journey in the world of making money online, the art of optimizing product listings and conversions is a skill that can significantly impact your bottom line. By implementing the strategies outlined in this subchapter, you can take your online business to new heights and achieve financial success in the digital realm.

Managing Inventory, Shipping, and Customer Service

In the ever-evolving world of online business, managing inventory, shipping, and customer service are crucial elements that can make or break your success. In this subchapter, we will explore effective strategies and best practices to ensure that these aspects of your online money-making venture are handled with utmost efficiency.

Inventory management is the backbone of any e-commerce operation. Whether you are selling physical products or digital goods, it is essential to keep track of your inventory levels to avoid stockouts or overstocking. Utilizing inventory management software can streamline this process, allowing you to monitor stock levels, generate reports, and automate reordering when necessary. By maintaining a well-organized and up-to-date inventory system, you can optimize your supply chain and minimize the risk of lost sales or excessive costs.

Shipping, on the other hand, plays a pivotal role in delivering your products to customers promptly and securely. Choosing the right shipping partners and methods is crucial to ensuring a smooth and reliable delivery experience. Consider factors such as shipping rates, delivery speed, and tracking capabilities when selecting your shipping options. Additionally, implementing a robust order fulfillment process, including packaging and labeling, will help to minimize errors and enhance customer satisfaction.

Customer service is the cornerstone of building trust and loyalty with your audience. Promptly addressing customer inquiries, resolving issues, and providing exceptional support can set you apart from your competitors. Establish clear communication channels, such as email, live chat, or phone support, and ensure that your team is well-trained to handle customer concerns effectively. Utilizing customer relationship management (CRM) software can help you centralize customer information, track interactions, and provide personalized service. In the online money-making landscape, customer feedback is invaluable. Encourage your customers to leave reviews and testimonials, as they not only provide social proof but also valuable insights for improvement. Actively monitoring customer feedback and addressing any negative reviews promptly can demonstrate your commitment to customer satisfaction. By efficiently managing inventory, shipping, and customer service, you can create a strong foundation for your online money-making venture. These aspects are essential for ensuring smooth operations, fostering customer loyalty, and maximizing profitability. Embrace the strategies and best practices outlined in this subchapter, and you will be well on your way to building a successful and sustainable online business.

Chapter 12: Scaling Your Online Business and Maximizing Profits

Strategies for Scaling and Growing Your Online Business

In the rapidly evolving digital landscape, scaling and growing an online business can seem like a daunting task. However, with the right strategies in place, you can take your venture to new heights and maximize your profits. This subchapter explores proven strategies tailored to various online business niches, including making money online, affiliate marketing, freelancing, dropshipping, online tutoring, social media management, blogging and content creation, online surveys and market research, virtual assistant services, selling digital products or courses, and e-commerce and online store management.

One of the most effective strategies for scaling your online business is to diversify your income streams. If you're solely relying on one niche, consider branching out into complementary areas. For example, if you're a successful affiliate marketer, explore opportunities to create and sell your own digital products or courses. This not only expands your revenue potential but also solidifies your expertise and brand.

Another strategy is to leverage social media platforms to build your online presence. Engage with your target audience, share valuable content, and establish yourself as an authority in your niche. This will help increase your visibility, attract more customers, and generate leads. Additionally, investing in social media management tools can streamline your efforts and provide valuable analytics to refine your marketing strategies.

Collaboration and partnerships can also fuel growth for your online business. Seek out like-minded individuals or businesses in your niche and explore opportunities to collaborate on projects or cross-promote each other's offerings. This not only expands your reach but also taps into the existing customer base of your partners.

Furthermore, optimizing your website for search engines is crucial for scaling your online business. Implement SEO strategies, such as keyword research, on-page optimization, and link building, to increase your organic traffic and improve your search engine rankings. This will result in higher visibility and more potential customers finding your website.

Lastly, as your online business grows, consider outsourcing tasks to virtual assistants. This allows you to focus on high-value activities and frees up your time for strategic decision-making. Virtual assistants can handle administrative tasks, customer support, content creation, and more, helping you scale your business efficiently.

By implementing these strategies, you can confidently scale and grow your online business while maximizing your profits. Remember, success doesn't happen overnight, but with dedication and perseverance, you can achieve your goals in the ever-expanding digital marketplace.

Automating and Outsourcing Tasks for Increased Efficiency

In today's fast-paced digital world, time is money. As an online entrepreneur or aspiring money maker, it is crucial to maximize your efficiency and productivity. This subchapter will delve into the strategies of automating and outsourcing tasks to streamline your online business and increase your potential for success.

One of the key benefits of running an online business is the ability to leverage automation tools. These tools can handle repetitive and time-consuming tasks, allowing you to focus on more important aspects of your business. Whether you're involved in affiliate marketing, freelancing, dropshipping, or any other online venture, automation tools can be a game-changer.

For instance, if you're engaged in social media management, you can utilize scheduling tools like Hootsuite or Buffer to automate your posts across various platforms. This will save you countless hours by eliminating the need to manually post content every day. Similarly, if you're a blogger or content creator, you can use content management systems like WordPress to automate tasks such as publishing, formatting, and even search engine optimization.

While automation tools are great, there are still tasks that require a human touch. This is where outsourcing comes into play. Outsourcing non-core tasks can free up your time to focus on revenue-generating activities. For example, if you're overwhelmed with managing customer inquiries or administrative work, hiring a virtual assistant could be a smart move. Virtual assistants can handle tasks like email management, data entry, research, and even social media engagement, allowing you to concentrate on more essential aspects of your business.

Outsourcing doesn't stop at virtual assistants; it extends to specialized services as well. If you're selling digital products or courses, you can outsource the creation of graphics, videos, or even the entire course development process. Additionally, for e-commerce and online store management, you can outsource inventory management, order fulfillment, and customer support, allowing you to focus on marketing and expanding your business.

In conclusion, automating and outsourcing tasks is essential for increased efficiency and productivity in the online money-making world. By leveraging automation tools and outsourcing non-core tasks, you can save time, reduce stress, and focus on revenue-generating activities. Whether you're a blogger, affiliate marketer, freelancer, or engaged in any other online niche, implementing these strategies will undoubtedly propel your success in the ever-evolving digital landscape. So, start harnessing the power of automation and outsourcing today, and watch your online business thrive.

Advanced Marketing and Sales Techniques

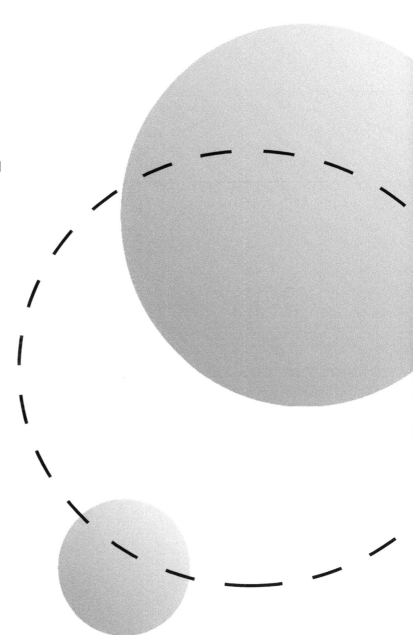

In today's digital era, the opportunities to make money online are endless. From affiliate marketing to e-commerce and online tutoring to social media management, there are various niches where individuals can thrive and achieve financial success. However, to truly maximize your potential in these fields, it is crucial to understand and implement advanced marketing and sales techniques. In this subchapter, we will delve into these strategies and equip you with the knowledge to excel in the online money-making world.

One of the most effective techniques in online marketing is personalization. By tailoring your marketing efforts to suit the needs and preferences of your target audience, you can significantly increase your conversion rates. This can be achieved through data analysis, customer segmentation, and creating personalized content or offers.

Furthermore, leveraging the power of social media platforms is essential in today's digital landscape. As a social media manager or blogger, you need to understand how to build a strong online presence, engage with your audience, and create compelling content that drives traffic and generates leads. Effective social media marketing involves utilizing various platforms, understanding algorithms, and staying up to date with the latest trends.

Additionally, content creation plays a pivotal role in attracting and retaining customers. Whether you are a blogger or an online tutor, producing high-quality, valuable content is key to building trust and credibility with your audience. Furthermore, incorporating search engine optimization (SEO) techniques in your content will help improve your visibility and organic reach.

Moreover, mastering the art of sales is crucial for success in any online money-making venture. Understanding the psychology of persuasion, utilizing persuasive copywriting techniques, and implementing effective sales funnels are all essential components of advanced sales techniques. By adopting these strategies, you can optimize your conversion rates and increase your revenue.

Lastly, staying ahead of the competition requires continuous learning and adaptation. As the online money-making landscape evolves rapidly, it is vital to keep up with the latest industry trends, tools, and strategies. Investing in your personal development and acquiring new skills will allow you to stay relevant and competitive in the market.

In conclusion, advanced marketing and sales techniques are instrumental in achieving success in the online money-making world. By personalizing your marketing efforts, leveraging social media platforms, creating valuable content, mastering sales techniques, and continuously learning and adapting, you can unlock your full potential and thrive in the niches of making money online, affiliate marketing, freelancing, dropshipping, online tutoring, social media management, blogging and content creation, online surveys and market research, virtual assistant services, selling digital products or courses, and e-commerce and online store management.

Maximizing Profits and Achieving Financial Freedom

In today's digital age, the opportunities to make money online are endless. Whether you're a seasoned entrepreneur or just starting out, the online world offers a plethora of avenues to explore and profit from. In this subchapter, we will delve into the strategies and tips that will help you maximize your profits and achieve the ultimate goal of financial freedom.

1. Understanding Your Niche: To effectively make money online, it's crucial to identify and understand your niche. Whether it's affiliate marketing, freelancing, dropshipping, or any other avenue, knowing your target audience and their needs will enable you to tailor your offerings and marketing strategies accordingly.

2. Creating Multiple Streams of Income: One of the keys to financial freedom is diversifying your income streams. Instead of relying on a single source, explore various opportunities like online tutoring, social media management, blogging, virtual assistant services, and selling digital products or courses. By diversifying, you'll not only maximize your profits but also mitigate risks associated with relying on a single income stream.

3. Building and Leveraging Your Online Presence: In the online world, your presence and reputation are everything. Utilize social media platforms, blogging, and content creation to establish a strong online presence. Engage with your target audience, provide valuable content, and build trust. This will not only attract more customers but also open doors to collaborations and partnerships, further boosting your profits.

4. Embracing E-commerce: With the rise of online shopping, e-commerce has become a lucrative field. Whether you choose to manage your own online store or utilize platforms like Amazon, eBay, or Shopify, e-commerce offers immense potential for profit. Learn the intricacies of product sourcing, inventory management, and customer service to optimize your e-commerce venture.

5. Optimizing Your Profitability: To maximize your profits, it's crucial to continuously analyze and optimize your strategies. Conduct market research, identify trends, and adapt your offerings accordingly. Explore the world of online surveys and market research to gain insights into consumer preferences and behavior. This will help you stay ahead of the competition and ensure sustained profitability.

6. The Power of Automation: As an online money maker, your time is valuable. Embrace automation tools and software to streamline your processes and save time. From email marketing automation to social media scheduling tools, automation can significantly increase your efficiency, allowing you to focus on income-generating activities.

In conclusion, maximizing profits and achieving financial freedom in the online world requires a combination of strategic thinking, adaptability, and perseverance. By understanding your niche, diversifying your income streams, building a strong online presence, embracing e-commerce, optimizing profitability, and utilizing automation, you can pave the way towards a financially independent future. So, seize the opportunities available to you and embark on your journey to online success!

Conclusion: Taking Action and Achieving Success in Making Money Online

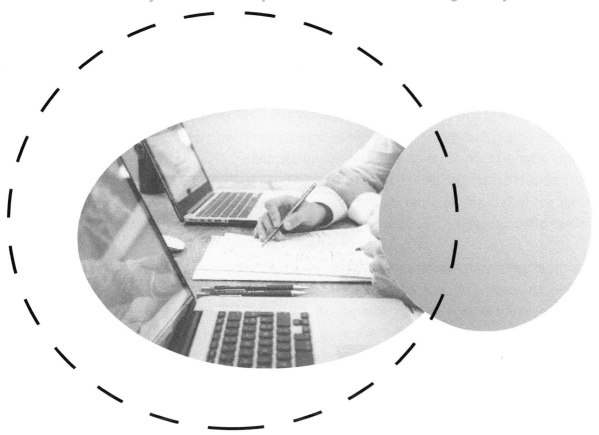

Congratulations! You have just embarked on an exciting journey towards financial freedom by exploring the vast world of making money online. Throughout this comprehensive guide, we have delved into various niches and strategies that can help you achieve success in the online money-making realm. Now, it's time to wrap up everything we have learned and provide you with the essential key takeaways to take action and excel in your online endeavors.

First and foremost, it is crucial to understand that success in making money online requires dedication, perseverance, and a willingness to step out of your comfort zone. While the online realm offers immense opportunities, it also demands continuous effort and a growth mindset. Keep in mind that overnight success stories are rare, and most successful online entrepreneurs have faced their fair share of challenges before reaching their goals.

One of the key lessons we have explored is the importance of selecting a niche that aligns with your passions, skills, and interests. Whether it's affiliate marketing, freelancing, dropshipping, online tutoring, social media management, blogging, or any other niche, choosing something you genuinely enjoy will give you the motivation and drive to excel in your efforts.

Furthermore, we have emphasized the significance of building a solid online presence. Establishing your brand through social media, content creation, and maintaining a professional website is essential for attracting clients, customers, and opportunities. Remember, consistency and quality are paramount in this digital landscape.

Additionally, we have discussed the various strategies for monetizing your online presence, such as selling digital products or courses, offering virtual assistant services, participating in online surveys and market research, or managing an e-commerce store. It's essential to explore multiple avenues and diversify your income streams to maximize your earning potential.

Lastly, we cannot stress enough the importance of continuous learning and staying updated with the latest trends and tools in the online money-making sphere. The digital landscape is ever-evolving, and to stay ahead of the competition, you must invest time and effort into expanding your knowledge and skillset.

In conclusion, making money online is a transformative journey that can lead to financial independence and personal growth. By taking action, staying committed, and applying the strategies we have discussed in this guide, you can pave the way towards a successful online career. Remember, success may not come overnight, but with dedication, perseverance, and the right mindset, you can achieve your goals and create a thriving online business. So, go forth, embrace the opportunities, and start your journey towards financial freedom today!

Milton Keynes UK
Ingram Content Group UK Ltd.
UKHW050621080324
438959UK00012B/467